OCCASIONAL DESIRE

OCCASIONAL DESIRE

Essays

DAVID LAZAR

University of Nebraska Press | Lincoln and London

Library of Congress Cataloging-in-Publication Data
Lazar, David, 1957–
[Essays. Selections]
Occasional desire: essays / David Lazar.
pages cm
ISBN 978-0-8032-4638-6 (pbk.: alk. paper)
I. Title.
PS3612.A973027 2013
814'.6—dc23   2013005456

Set in Fanwood Text by Laura Wellington.
Designed by A. Shahan.

That is true wisdom, to know how
to alter one's mind when occasion
demands it.

TERENCE

Whenever evil befalls us, we ought to
ask ourselves, after the first suffering,
how we can turn it into good. So shall
we take occasion, from one bitter root,
to raise perhaps many flowers.

LEIGH HUNT

CONTENTS

OCCASIONAL DESIRE

UNFAMILIAR ESSAYS

CALLING FOR HIS PAST

Public telephones were a specific genre, a public genre, lacking the cool control of environment of the private phone. This was especially true in cities of public exuberance, where passersby were apt to insert themselves into the lives before them. Freud says there are never only two people in bed, and just so, there were rarely only two people on public telephones in New York. The silent stares of those waiting for the phone, accusing the user of an offensive lack of brevity, the casual interruptions of those walking by, their conversational inflections counterpointing one's own, and the occasional pure interruption (I once had a woman wrestle the phone out of my hand in frustration, once had a man fix me with a look and imperiously command me to "Say good-bye") all conspired with the ever-present participant—the city itself, its horns and rumbles, screeches and weathers—to diminish the intensity of the solitary voice and make its attempts at communication precarious. Intensifying these difficulties was the fact that public calls were so frequently generated by some exigency of time or fault in planning. As such, pay phones were magnets of confusion; their products: artifacts of arrangement that could deconstruct as they were being made, the street name blurred, the time obscured.

3

My specific fascination with public phones began at a movie theater in Brooklyn, one of the old, cavernous, pre-prefabricated variety, when I was seven or eight. These ornate miniature opera houses had fallen on hard times and were usually sparsely attended, a few pockets of moviegoers dotting the vacant landscape of seats. But far from forlorn, one could explore the wide-open spaces of the hall as though urged on by a manifest destiny of vision, finding the right seat for the right film, a suitable distance from the other settlers, preferably close enough to let the screen fill in the entire plot of sight. From the earliest age, I craved an encompassing rather than a comprehensive view of movie screens. I wanted to feel taken as I took it in. I had been deposited at a Saturday matinee and was calling home to confirm the details of who would pick me up and to inform them of my estimated time of arrival into the late summer afternoon. Before plugging in my dime, I checked the coin return and was rewarded with a slim gold wedding band. Too young to imagine the dimensions of the tragic or melodramatic scene that had engendered my surprise, I still had a glimmer of drama and a sense that the ring had been magically bestowed on me. Nevertheless, in the realm of the wonderful, I performed the expected, discharging my obligation of honor by reporting the find to the manager, the guardian of gate receipts, a gentleman of seventeen or so, who irked my wonder with his casual "Keep it, kid," as though such discoveries were commonplace. Did rings show up in phone booths all the time, a quotidian gesture of a world where marriage and movies were somehow linked? Had I been rudely kept in the dark about this missing link of courtship? I resisted the idea that this was not a signal, a gesture to me from an unknown source, some phone deity, the operative voice of God. In a feminized version of Arthur and Excalibur, I had been the one to pull the ring from slot, and I left in triumph with my tiny bottomless Grail and the incipient belief that anything can happen at the movies and in phone booths.

This mystery was followed by a later encounter of the "found" world of public telephones. "Phil Abbate keeps calling for his past," the note said, by the telephone on Greenwich Avenue, in Greenwich Village, thirty years ago. Someone had left it in the space between the bottom of the phone and the hopelessly useless small silver shelf underneath. So I waited there; I wanted to see if he would call again. And I thought, if Abbate did call, what could I tell him? That it was getting dark? That the traffic was light and the shadow of the library was inching toward the phone? Not knowing him would put me in a poor position to answer any but the most extraneous questions. I waited again. I began to think it might be an elaborate joke conceived by some baroque society of Village Pierrots. Perhaps they wanted to test how long some enigma-starved pedestrian would wait to get his Phil. Was there such a thing as a found practical joke? How passive, almost Eastern. There I stayed, twenty minutes, forty minutes, waiting for a fellow to call for his past. He didn't call; I gave up the vigil, but the note came with me, folded in half, housed in a back apartment of my wallet. I showed it around, but friends tended to be dubious, wary of my instigation of this strange little fiction: "Isn't the writing just a little like yours," they would smirk. "Those childish loping loops?" This was plainly nonsense since the writing was firm, almost elegant, not the slightest like my own. One friend decided to decode it when the throes of my speculation were at their peak. She directed my attention to the Greek root of "Phil," *philo*, love; and what I had been pronouncing as an Italian surname, A-bate, could be read as the plain "abate." Presto, the note was surely announcing that love abates and keeps calling for its past, a recondite epigrammatic note in a bottle. I considered this vision: the phone as bottle, the note as note, and I the heroic urban scavenger of telephone shores. But this reading collapsed like a house of notes thanks to her cynical version of the text, which cast me as the complete auteur: as bottle, as note, foisting the message on the rest of the world, as me. Doesn't anyone enjoy a good mystery? I returned to the question of Phil Abbate calling for his past, on occasion would briefly stake out the phone, waiting for his ring to return. It never did. But the note did yield another clue, a clue to the way I think. My mind finally turned from the message to the medium, the figure I had avoided entirely, who might be saying to himself, herself, even now, that Phil Abbate kept calling for his past, even now with more years of past to call for, the burden heavier, more complicated. Was it the mother of Phil, Mater Dolorosa, leaving a testament to her martyred son? Old flame who left it in frustration at Phil's insistent, pathetic nostalgia? Or another passerby, creating a chain of sympathy for a random call in search of the past, preparing his substitute for the demands of this phone? Realizing I had an accomplice, another disciple of Phil's vague misfortune, was a relief if not a rescue from obsession, since I still think of Phil, embracing a future as dark as Faust, with Bell his Mephistopheles, calling here and there for his past.

Perhaps my inability to resist ringing pay phones was inspired by Phil Abbate, but I no longer have any hope of meeting his voice. The ringing pay phone was the stray dog of communication, the aural image of urban alienation that called out on some crowded street or in the middle of a crowd-filled day, when perhaps you had spoken to no one, that you could speak to someone, that a voice was waiting for a number, that even a wrong answer was a salve for silence. And there was that most unusual condition of answering with complete anonymity. You could say anything, confess, if you desired, your most heinous crimes, most lingering guilts, without the danger of being traced. Dangling as an option, of course, was the perverse possibility of dangerous fun, of answering the phone and committing your most heinous crimes. Since my phone falls of many years ago, I've never thought of the receiver in quite the same way.

New York in the Thirties, that is the East Thirties, somewhere around midnight. I was living on the other coast, had come to town to visit, to Manhattan for a rendezvous with friends, a couple who had also entered the diaspora that awaits most ex–New Yorkers. We had met at his mother's apartment, always seemed to gravitate there when we converged. His mother was a gentle woman; she was quite, but not completely, deaf. Years of exclusion from conversation, from the sequence of words and the substance of sentences, had made her apt to insert proclamations that were rarely appropriate to the subject, but seemed to give her an illusion of being included. On my visits, we tried to keep her current with our talk, but invariably the quick rhythms of conversation carried us past her. We had spent a giddy evening indulging in nostalgic reminiscences in the tone of old jokes. We found ourselves snacking on creamed herring and crackers in the garishly bright kitchen light. We agreed it was much too bright for herring. Mrs. Gitmann took on a look of intense concentration, not unlike the pained concentration of a child relieving himself in public. She meant to speak. She issued forth two statements: "I love all the fish in the ocean," meaning she loved to eat them, and "The herring is a good fish," which we later agreed had sounded like approbation. We followed our mostly stifled laughter onto the balcony for a guilty paroxysm of laughter, laughing out into the night and over the Catholic girls' school on Lexington Avenue. One of the sisters gazed unmercifully out at us from her little lit window, restoring us to guilty sobriety. It was time to leave.

The Third Avenue Thirties was a disturbing place to walk at night thirty years ago, when it had no life at all, no one on the streets, the since departed automat a depopulated Hopper with little lit windows, a Nun I thought, in every one, and the still faraway glitter of the Upper East Side, where I would enter the last station of the crosstown train.

The phone rang, a welcome delay and distraction. A man's voice, gruff and provocative, said "Lemme speak to Linda." I was already edgy and found his unmannerliness highly annoying. I engaged before I knew what I was doing. I said, "Linda can't come to the phone right now. Who is calling?" I could almost feel the wind sucked out of him. Dumbfounded, he retorted, "Who's this? Who the fuck are you? Put Linda on the phone." His lack of humor seemed oddly intolerable in the face of my own bad faith. Reaching back into the school yard, I said, "Look, Linda doesn't want to talk to you, so how about shaving your knuckles and sleeping it off." He ended our sequence of delightful repartees by informing me that he and his cronies were coming over to break my legs, and hung up before I could interrupt (would I have in fact interrupted?) and inform him that Linda was not really with me on the corner of Thirty-Sixth and Third. Even so, I felt I had to move on before the gang pinioned me by the phone. So I had progressed from mea culpa to mea maxima culpa. I also carried away, repeated like a novena, the most fervent prayer that my faux mistress could talk on her feet before he got to her legs.

Learning from experience has never been my strong suit. At times, I feel like a walking rebuke to behaviorism. Thirty-three years ago, I lived briefly in Manhattan, in a minute studio apartment on Fifty-Seventh Street, west of First Avenue. It always let in just enough light and noise to keep an awareness of the city maddeningly handy. I would hear pieces of conversation, juxtaposed bits of pedestrianism: "It's just like the old job . . . gonna pour in a minute . . . they have those in Jersey?" It was a nightmare of, a penance for, Mrs. Gitmann. At night I would hear more intriguing fragments from prostitutes returning from their shift. These were rendered even more surreal when they woke me from deep sleep, my waking punctuated by incomprehensible sexual prisms of talk. To keep madness at bay, I often wandered out, even if not very far. On one outing, I had barely gone two blocks, when the phone on the corner of Fifty-Eighth and First called to me with an alarming, a brash, a beseeching ring. My earlier experience had informed me of the need for tact and sensitivity; it certainly did not demand that I avoid what would be, were it not for me, local calls to limbo. Besides, after living in that studio apartment for months, I felt it was my right to talk back to the city, to infect it with my own benign voice. I picked up the phone, answered in the tone of a bon vivant:

ME: Good evening.
VOICE: Hello.
ME: Who's calling?
VOICE: I can . . . I see you.
        I thought his stutter meant, "could I see you," a
        truly blind date.
ME: Well, I'm spoken for, but flattered and charmed
        nevertheless.
VOICE   (WITH MORE AUTHORITY): I can see you down
        there on the corner. Fifty-Eighth.
ME   (SKEPTICAL, TESTING): And what do I look like?
        Where are you?
VOICE: Aren't you afraid down there by yourself? Is that
        why you're looking up for me?

I thought of threatening to break his legs. I considered calling for my past. But the phone clicked, and I hurried away, back to my tiny box, figuring anyone who could pay for a high-rise could undoubtedly make payments on a long-range rifle.

My pay phone experiences have all but evaporated since then. I still long for the beckoning ring. My expectations are depressed. But I'm not completely cynical. No one who passes by what remains of public telephones with a glimmer of hope for serendipity is completely without hope, layered in a sense of the improbable. On our worst days, I might confess, we are the aural equivalents of peeping toms, urban eavesdroppers, if a little less passive. There is always the chance of seeing and hearing what we wish we were immune to. Think of James Stewart in *Rear Window*. Who could have known that Raymond Burr was so bad? And Baudelaire on his walks around Paris. He might as well have been answering pay phones when he wrote:

Indignant as a drunk who sees the world
double, I staggered home and locked my door,
scared and sick at heart and scandalized
that so much mystery could be absurd!

Vainly my reason sought to take the helm

("The Seven Old Men")

He understands that the streets are full of madness, as were its phones, but even so both were sometimes better than going home alone.

MANHATTAN CAB

James Agee and Robert Lowell both died in taxis in New York. Neither writer compels a strong association with New York. Death is another matter. But Lowell's line from his last book, "The light at the end of the tunnel / Is the light of the oncoming train," takes me into the Brooklyn Battery Tunnel, my lifeline into Manhattan and back home to Brooklyn for so many years. In zone five of the tunnel (were my first crude metaphysical meditations inspired by the tunnel's zones, speculations about their depth, length, their separation?), light would snake around the last curve before Manhattan. As a child, I would sometimes imagine a behemoth waiting there, breathing fire, jaws ready to split the car, swallow it, or burn it. For years, zone five was the fire zone, the danger zone. What I see now, when I very occasionally make that drive on a visit, is no less disheartening: light from the city I abandoned years ago, the uncertain light of never having made terms with it. My automotive navigations echo this: where to turn, where to park, the knowledge of which had been instinctual. Agee, Lowell, I cannot even take a taxi in Manhattan, afraid as I am of the meter, the curb, and short stops.

ACROSS THE RIVER

By the time I was eleven or twelve, I started making semiweek-
ly trips into Manhattan, first with Billy Meylach, later on with
Rob Steele or Greg Uzoaga. Greg's parents, strangely enough,
were a high school principal and the treasurer of Nigeria—or
so Greg said. I had spoken on the phone with his mother, and
she sounded like a principal. As for his father, I thought it rather an elaborate occupation, but don't remember questioning its
veracity. After all, this was Brooklyn; parents did all kinds of
things, and I suppose a Nigerian treasurer sounded no less plausible than a distributor of customized rivets, or a manufacturer
of cut-rate doll apparel, or a butcher who specialized in tongue.
In any case, I mention my friends' names—hopefully not to their
dismay—because they give me so much pleasure to say. Sometimes, when I'm looking at old pictures, the pleasure blurs from
visual to verbal, the faces become icons for the names: Primavera, Petrocini, Lissoon, Migliaro, Sugarman, Wasserman, and
Schactman. Of course that's Primavera! Who could that be but
Sugarman? What's in a name? Sometimes I think everything.

In any case, on our sojourns, there were certain things we'd always do, rituals of visitation. There used to be a Ripley's Be-

lieve It or Not! museum on Broadway, around Forty-Seventh Street, I believe. There were displays, not well-kept, of all kinds of freakishness, dusty freakishness and smeared glass, the most unbelievable of the believe-them-or-nots. They rarely had anything to do with the city, with what we knew. This was where the fascination lay to a great extent. Freak animals, freak men, and freak women, all seemed to share certain basic qualities: they mated unnaturally, performed the physiologically impossible, or were mini-Jobs, surviving or not through travails that made us less squeamish about the Forty-Second Street station and our own magnified growing pains. There were occasionally freak objects, as well, but they generally had at least a tenuous connection to the malformed, the maledicted. I cannot recall what we did or did not actually believe. That was beside the point. It was all a test of suspension of disbelief, some almost teasingly possible, some seemingly beyond the pale, all challenging credibility with the nonchalance of "believe it, or not, we don't really care how dully tied to terra firma you are." The moral imperative to believe balanced with our sense of dignity, our fear of gullibility. I think my favorite displays were dioramas of the quotidian pushed to the absurd. Eating an egg was certainly familiar enough. But the Australian who mysteriously started eating them one morning and couldn't stop until he had devoured 373 boiled eggs? I believe the display unfathomably centered around, yes, an egg. Or the dog in Andalusia who had a forty-seven-foot hairball pulled out of him (the numbers were always odd for credibility's sake). As a zaftig kid, I believe the subgenre of the familiar gone mad that usually hooked me most were eating binges, frenzies, or, in the rare case, aristeias. They seemed—these narratives—to form a queasy blend of the revolting and the charming. The man who ate only sticks. The woman who ate chocolate twenty hours out of every day until she turned, of course, a deep shade of cocoa, just this side of Josephine Baker. Or what about the little boy—this was getting perilously close—who weighed 189 pounds at the age of eight? There was nothing better for the morale of those who felt freakish than to see their truly freakish betters. Except, of course, on those bad days when the kinship seemed not so strained, when one thought, I bet I could eat chocolate for, let's say, six hours a day, and when one's reflection hit the glass and one saw oneself superimposed into one's own box of unique grossness, weirdness, believe-it-or-notness. I'm the boy who . . . but surely no one could stand to look at that.

Next, we would go to the arcade down the street. Two rituals were always performed here, and we experienced them as shamanistic confirmations of our tour of the Manhattan underworld. We had plastic medals printed with our names or catchy phrases or private messages to each other scrolled around the perimeter. These medallions, I noticed, were still being pressed and pitched at the Empire State Building several years ago. I had taken my wife for her first visit there, and she thought these kiddy souvenirs cute in a kitschy kind of way. I rolled my eyes at what had become of the hard currency of our picaresque voyages, forgetting of course that these little tokens of remembrance were always the essence of kitsch. But I like to take my kitsch straight these days, no chaser. And I hate the feeling of embarrassment at formerly glorious prized possessions. That's why if I'm going to see or have kitsch now, I want to own it as a newly embraced thing, not an old guilty pleasure. You can't go home again, to kitsch.

My friends and I always asked questions of the fortune-telling machine, which contained a doll-sized woman, a Gypsy, a *gallitzeana*, my father would have said (the Romanian cast of aspersion clinging to it). She was surrounded by plate glass and served as a bridge from Ripley's, could have been an exhibit on loan, in fact: world's smallest woman mummified by relatives. She had glassy eyes that seemed to endow her with more occult knowledge than any other glassy-eyed person I've met, in or out of a vending machine. We taunted her uneasily, saying, "Hey, toots, you have a sister," and, "I bet you say that to all the boys." However, speaking for myself (an enterprise I've sometimes had enough trouble with), this usually felt like sacrilege within two or three minutes. And if you're going to go to the trouble of learning your future from a machine, it would seem foolhardy to provoke it into becoming a mad *machina*. Unless I'm mistaken, everything she foretold has proven true, up to and including the then enigmatic line foretelling that I would go very far, yet stay very close.

Next stop, headlines, newspaper front pages printed up to order. These were most fun when they glorified ourselves or made fools out of friends and relatives: DAD GIVEN TICKER TAPE PARADE, or LEO (my father) WHISPERS, WORLD ASTONISHED. The place where we made these always quickly disposed-of purchases was sorry, old; you could smell it in the ink from the mechanical presses, the obliviousness of the owner sensing his own anachronism. Men in run-down, anachronistic businesses in New York in the 1960s always seemed to have the air of a Borscht Belt comedian who had gotten tired of telling jokes. They always seemed on the verge of saying something, before saying nothing. Whenever I chance to use the word "desultory," I think of a dimly lit business that has seen better days, or perhaps just other days. I thought of the Times Square newspaper shop years later when reading Balzac's description of the Sechard press in *Lost Illusions*. But in this store there weren't fond memories of a lost time; it looked as though it had always existed in some older world. I always locate their building where the half-price ticket center for Broadway shows is in New York, near Herald Square, but that can't be right; there was never any building there. I realize I do that with New York. I'm not quite sure where certain old buildings, stores, restaurants were, but I am comfortable finding a place that seems right for them to have been. And that is where I construct my invisible architectural mausoleums. In any case, the sign above the print shop read PRINT YOUR NAME HERE, the perfect invocation of transience.

Our final stop would usually be Rockefeller Center, where, if we were lucky and early, we could snag some tickets for a TV game show from one of the poor, ever-cheerful young men who dispersed them to tourist types, many of whom drifted languidly and officiously away from the solicitation, as though they had been told to avoid contact with anyone in New York who approaches you. On one show, they were giving prizes to audience members whose birthday it was. The qualification was to answer some perfectly banal question, which I felt, on one occasion, more than qualified for. I went up to take my chances and, pressed for verification, informed the master of ceremonies that it was my not my birthday but my father's (well, a couple of weeks earlier). I must have assumed they wouldn't quibble in front of a crowd when confronted with such a spunky young charmer. Still, thinking back, I'm amazed at my apparent confidence at this semiscam, this pseudoheisting of literal truth, and its accompaniment by honesty. Why lie, and then why own up? The propulsive desires and ethical quandaries of childhood. I always think of myself as having been retiring, a genteel lad, until some effluvium from the past, some prima facie bit of evidence, proves me dead wrong. In any case, the bastards gave me zilch. I returned to my seat in the audience as a humiliated little liar, determined to feel oppressed by the cultural forces of meaninglessness. Of course, in truth, getting something on the sly wasn't entirely out of bounds for my familial training, which stressed results over process, with a healthy dose of scorn for an overcommitment to playing by the rules. I think this (a)moral seasoning dogged me for years, bogged me down until I realized—I can locate this precisely as having occurred somewhere between the ages of twenty and thirty—that I performed best on all occasions when I stuck to the rules, played it fair instead of loose. To cast glibness aside, the point is that I was trained to think that in the city, your wits should lead you to victory, to getting what you want and need, that savvy slight dishonesty was what you cleverly used or were trumped by. How disheartening, dispiriting, and (I sense one more coming) disillusioning to realize that my skill in almost all cases resided in the reasonably honest use of intellect, emotion, and language. In short, I think I was duped into thinking that I could dupe. What a rube; how city-humiliating to be so self-trumped.

From Rockefeller Center we would walk downtown on Sixth Avenue to Thirty-Fourth Street to catch the D or F train back to Brooklyn. Sometimes we would stop at my father's office on Thirty-Third and Seventh. The view was striking: he overlooked Madison Square Garden, Penn Station, Seventh Avenue, from the tenth floor. The business was a travel agency, but the office was vintage Garment District: messy, crowded, raucous, without the amenities one associates with thriving businesses, secretaries or doorbells, or a modicum of organization. It was unpolished and aggressively friendly to all but those who wandered in cold (the audacity!). In other words, the office of Comet Travel—manned by its Jewish proprietor, Italian First Lieutenant Vinny, and whatever intransigent clerk who could bear the pressure and mayhem for the short term—was a metaphor for the city: full of pressure, comedy, and focused hospitality. The insults flew fast and furious, ethnically based of course; and the theatrical would spike an appearance rather frequently in the form of unmitigated, raging anger on the phone. I couldn't count the times that my father (usually) or Vinny (occasionally) would tear into an airline functionary about some mistake in ticketing that threatened to put the kibosh on an expensive ticket. Is this kind of business anger—the unvarnished, semiobscene name-calling brutishness that was all in a day's work—a thing of the past? Of course, having experienced some of my father's anger firsthand muted some of the delight in seeing Olympian anger freely vented. I would watch and listen with a combination of admiration and horror as my father berated his object of scorn, his accidental impediment to the processing of a lucrative tick-et. I realize that I've said nary a word about my companions on these trips (for good reason, I don't really remember their com-pany—the city and its days though ring back loud and clear), but if a friend had joined me for the jaunt, as was usual, I would have to explain that the hollering was all in a day's work. I do remember, vaguely, some startled delight from a friend or two when my father would slam down the phone—"Go fuck your-self; we'll see about that!"—and greet us warmly without miss-ing a beat. "You kids have a good day?" "Yeah, but it was pretty hot." "Good, see you home later." "So long, Dad."

Either train would do for the ride home to Brooklyn. The F would take us to Avenue X or Stillwell Avenue, depending on what we had in mind: food in the former, vagrancy the latter. The D was the preferred route. It was faster and traveled through areas of Flatbush and Midwood that I felt strangely nostalgic about then, perhaps the sense of neighborhoods in desultory transition. Perhaps my mother's stories of strolling around beau-tiful Flatbush neighborhoods in the summers in the 1940s (echoes of James Agee . . .). But Sheepshead Bay was the real reason for the D choice. Through the years, it had become identified as our station, the one where I waited with my mother in the car for my father to emerge down from the elevated platform, past the newspaper stand that was always open; and it seemed the hardiest and most dependable institution known to man. We would bet on which train he was on. Betting on time is a practice in my family that neither anger, death, nor years of separation have put a stop to. I sometimes think that when I tell my family in October that I'll be home in December, lottery sales drop precipitously. Sometimes my father would call from the station and walk down Avenue Z toward the oncoming cars, to save time. Were that the case, he would call and hurriedly exclaim "Sheepshead Bay!" into the receiver, hanging up in time to get his dime back.

I, too, would sometimes call from the station ("call from the station" was to our family a "see you later" line, an out the door line). But usually my friend and I would walk down Avenue Z, past the Chinese restaurant whose door was open, giving us the whiff of generic Chinese restaurant, past the middle-income housing projects, the brick Brooklyn that is always the Brooklyn I think about first, past the "beverage place" that delivered our seltzer, past my mother's seamstress who pinioned me with pins, past the school three blocks from home that I never attended and whose name I was never sure of (were we hiding from each other?), its paddleball courts and stickball players in the inner school yard, the school garden usually gone to weeds where the rubber balls ended up, past the one-family semiattached "units" that bordered Z and Ocean Parkway and were rumored to have been "slummy" since the first day they were occupied. When you live in a row house you're keenly aware of the gradations of class represented by how housing is kept up. There, a right turn for me, two blocks down Ocean Parkway, "between Y and Z" we would say to visitors as an aid to navigation that sounded unimprovably precise. More precise would have been the short block between Brighton and Manhattan Court.

Brighton Court, the last leg of the trip, the picaresque's penultimate street, was always a thrill to pass. For years, it was a Dionysian zone to me. I'm not sure if this began or confirmed my feeling, but one Halloween, trick-or-treating, I rang the bell of a dark house, blinds drawn, all supernaturally quiet. I rang and summoned the improbable. (Shouldn't the appearance of the unrepressed be a sister concept to the return of the repressed?) A beautiful young woman in a black negligee answered. "What do you want?" she asked. Not with hostility or unbecoming seductiveness. It was a serious and pleasant inquiry, so pleasant my ten- or twelve-year-old self was all shaken up as I ran and ran and ran home, thrilled. And I thought about her for years, and never went back. She was always part of my little shiver, my sense of something dark out there that had, sometime later, to be explored in the last block, the buzz of Brooklyn in see-through black, where for better and worse, the most visceral doors always opened and closed and crossing the river meant always crossing back.

THE CITY ALWAYS SPEAKS

LONDON, NEW YORK, SAN FRANCISCO

But sidewalks and those who use them are not passive
beneficiaries of safety or helpless victims of danger. Sidewalks, their bordering uses, and their users, are active
participants in the drama of civilization versus barbarism in
cities. . . . The bedrock attribute of a successful city district is
that a person must feel personally safe and secure on the
street among all these strangers. . . . To be sure, there are
people with hobgoblins in their heads, and such people will
never feel safe no matter what the objective circumstances
are . . . there must be a clear demarcation between what
is public space and what is private space . . . there must be
eyes upon the street.

JANE JACOBS, *The Death and Life of Great American Cities*

Despite all my desires for it not to, violence has defined what I
have known about where I have been.

In London thirty years ago, a friend and I were on our way
back to the Indian hotel we were camped in a few blocks from
Victoria Station. The pervasive smell of Indian cooking, so delightful for chosen repasts, was dizzyingly exotic. We both had

hot swirling dreams; we woke into curried sweats. Consequently, we spent little time in our little room.

It was Saturday night. A few streets past the station was one of those zoning quirks, urban way stations, close in fact to a weigh station: docks of lorries loading and unloading crates of what used to be called, generically, goods. We saw a young man and woman arguing violently. A few of the men who had been loading, unloading, decided to watch as well. We were united by voyeurism with a dash of concern for the girl's safety. The young man kept trying to pull the girl with him, but each time, she resisted furiously and smacked him in the head, punched him in the chest. Our sympathies became confused (the city scene as B movie: whom does one root for?), but we were afraid that the young man, who began bloodying himself by hitting his head on a brick wall after every episode of the girl's vehement resistance, was going to erupt at some point. Sure enough, he reached his limit of inspired self-abuse and started pummeling the girl, belting her furiously in the stomach, the way come-from-behind boxers do in old movies. The girl screamed, which seemed to amuse the lorry men, but responding to our own ingrained siren sound, we raced over to the two. I pulled the boy off, and my larger and more physically capable friend gripped him in a paralyzing upper-body lock.

The young man attempted to struggle, desultorily, for a minute or two, out of fear. To him our intervention must have felt at first like a random assault. He may have seen red, his blood on our clothes, as confusing to him, no doubt, as it was casually disgusting to us.

He pitched into a drunken epiphany, thanking us profusely for stepping in, imploring us to come and drink with him, "on me, on me, all on me." The girl, who had scattered, returned, almost sauntering back into the picture. We asked her to go home. She walked to the end of the street and waited. We released the boy, since our detention had reached a kind of silly standstill. He joined the girl; they turned the corner.

Our adrenaline was still racing, and we walked back to the hotel with a strange sense of elation, as though delighting both in the efficacy of our involvement and its parodic denouement. What had begun as voyeurism, the prerogative of travelers, ended up as our most engaged moment of the week. Home or abroad, perhaps that is what the *flaneur* is seeking: an excuse to interact with the city, the desire for impulse covered by the necessity of compulsion.

London, 1985

"Bitch, bitch!" A boy, about seven, wearing a white fisherman's sweater, backing away from his mother or nanny, but pushing into the words as he speaks them. Moving into and away from the words simultaneously. She implores Gerald to "come here now and be good." The part of Gerald moving backward into the world wants to be good, but Gerald has discovered the power of language. He sees through his companion's falsely cool and reasonable demeanor, into the heart that wants to shake the boy, to pulverize him into civility. His vulnerability keeps him poised in the rhythmic balance, backward and forward. The pose of her poise terrifies him. The street is in Hampstead, upscale. This scene is not an unusual affair, apparently, to the shoppers. Most confirm their discomfort, however, by their tactful refusal to acknowledge the confrontation. But Gerald is a little anarchist, terrorist; he wants to tear the street apart, scream the world into submission. "Bitch, bitch!" Gerald is using up her patience, and his power, since he has no other shocking words, no reserves. Nevertheless, I am as surprised as Gerald when she strides forward and strikes him across the face, and I remain surprised, frozen into a tactless stare, that Gerald does not crumple and crumble quite as fast as a small boy might, with his small power deprived. I think to myself, I would have sworn it hurt like a bitch. The ironies language leads us to are inevitable, but unavailable to Gerald. When a large hand and a small word duke it out, hand wins hands down. I blink, and he is being led away. In the late afternoons in cities, the captive and the captured are joined in their capitulations to form.

London, 1988

Overheard on the Northern Line:

SHE: What are you thinking about?
HE: I was wondering what you were thinking about.
SHE: Me too.

Understood by the eavesdropper: The couple is on a cusp, being prodded to jump onto the tracks of metalove by the little amourvore on their shoulders, the grim reaper who tells them their emerging self-consciousness is charming and knows, to boot, that no one will risk saying what's really on his or her mind. The safest response can lead to romantic carnage.

Twice in San Francisco, the city seemed to be acting out its own supernatural urban id. I was living in Palo Alto thirty years ago. My girlfriend suggested we drive up to the city to see a newly released 3-D version of *Dial M for Murder*. I felt like saying we'd never make it to New York by evening.

The theater, since closed, was in the Mission District. It was one of those enormous old caves, its splendor removed gradually over the years in the conversion to hollow hall. We parked about a block away. It was strange enough to sit among perhaps five hundred people wearing 3-D glasses, but about halfway through the film (I like to think during a close-up of Ray Milland) the theater started swaying. We all knew what that meant. There was some nervous mumbling in response, but no one left; the crowd responded abashedly to two or three snarling imprecations for quiet. True Californian film buffs, I thought: the earth moved, but no one else did. The show went on.

Afterward, we emerged to find that my car had been robbed: front windows broken, radio ripped out. A ghastly assortment of wires protruded from the dash, making it look like those movie images of bodies with their heads ripped off. But when I saw the broken window from a distance, my first irrational response was that the earthquake had done it. And when I saw the wires, for a brief instant I wondered how the shifting plates of the earth had carried off my radio. The revenge of Orpheus? We drove down the peninsula in silence, Hefty bags taped around the windows, smoke from the recesses of the smashed center dash blowing in our faces. The next day, my mechanic informed me that the passenger window had been merely rolled down. Years later, in a chance reencounter, I ran into my ex-companion in New York. She confided in me that, contrary to my movement from the irrational to the quotidian truth, she had eventually come to believe that the earthquake had in fact vandalized the car, ended our relationship, and worsened her eyesight significantly. She had the laugh of someone who has had too much therapy, and needs much more. I had the ironic smirk of same. We both confessed our love for cities and parted casually, as though still in the grip of some unsettlingly, unmotivated power.

Some months later, I was in San Francisco's Chinatown when a car full of young Chinese men tried to cut me off from the parking lane. I exercised the rightness of my way and speeded up, effectively cutting them off. I have come to realize that this was a specific mistake, a poorly chosen moment for pedagogical driving. The driver caught up with me and spun his car around, blocking my way. Before I could put my car into the phantom sixth gear, flee, he was out and approaching my car, followed by three or four other young men, spitting on my hood and kicking my door, trying vainly to pry me out. I was struck by the gesture of spitting at a car; one forgets how personalized they are to some. However, my response was not Sicilian umbrage at this honor-challenging defacement but horror at the look of faces spitting out curses, the silent and cinematic grotesqueness of those raging contortions that are the product of casual near accidents. I veered and spun my way out of there somehow, dodging down some side streets for the sake of safe passage and the satisfaction of an old demand that the object of flight circumnavigate. My door was dented in twenty places; my car was not pretty. But it is the quiet violence of those faces I remember most, the snarling impotence of a life of scores to settle.

In the winter of 1971 my brother and I went to see James Taylor at Madison Square Garden, our home away from home thanks to years of Knicks home games. The city always seemed safer in winter, fewer people on the street. Summer was hassle time. We were in the mall of the Garden, perhaps fifty feet from the entrance, but had gotten separated by the mob, the crowd I suppose one should say these days. The Mafia had no controlling interest in folk music at the time, as far as I know. Two teenagers, one much smaller than I, sandwiched me. The smaller one matter-of-factly told me to give him a dollar. He didn't beseech or demand. He was giving me a simple, calm command. Unfortunately, after a childhood of endless payoffs to a variety of child thugs, I had reached an age or stage where I would not give money readily to anyone more than three inches shorter than I. I figured the situation favored a refusal. After all, we were in the mall, the foyer of our second home. I said no, almost as matter-of-factly as the demand had been made, though with a slight intonation that implied a note of irony, a kind of noblesse oblige that suggested, "Little fellow, I find the tenor of your request ill-advised and positively unreasonable." I turned and the short guy rabbit-punched me so hard that I was actually out for a few seconds—the only time in my life when I've had the Bogey "What hit me?" experience, which is, I suppose, a form of violent anesthesia. I found myself on the floor, my brother hovering over with the automatic smile we both assume for serious trouble or pain. My head throbbed, and my eye was swollen and cut on the side. My assailant had been wearing a ring. I sat through the opening act with an ice pack on my eye. Shortly after Taylor came on, I started having muscle spasms in my thigh. I remember little of the concert except for my unwavering determination to enjoy myself and, going back to Brooklyn, the survivor's sense of painful empowerment—the testament of war wounds—that alternated with a sense of extreme stupidity, having gotten too much for my money.

Five years later, I was again on my way to the Garden, to meet my parents for a Knicks game. I was in a corner seat on the D train, my line, just shy of Prospect Park. Five teenagers came through from the other car, scoped out my quarter-filled car, and gathered around me, one taking the seat to my right. One kid asked for the time; it was 5:20. I knew I was going to miss my watch, but a graduate student from Columbia had been stabbed to death on the D train the week before. I was hoping I could lose my timepiece and save my time life. My seat neighbor asked for watch and wallet. I surprised myself by asking for the wallet back, sans bucks. Struck by the novelty of the idea, they obliged. But what followed has always stayed with me most. At Prospect Park one of the gang held the door open while the others insisted on shaking my hand.

I instantly despised the pusillanimity of the man and woman who solicited my well-being once the doors were closed. They came up to me and said, "Are you OK? Are you all right?" I said, "Fuck you," felt friendlier to my five white-collar wannabe robbers. Solicitude is meant to happen before the doors are closed. I informed the conductor and met the police at the next stop. My one experience with mug shots was to end lugubriously when I went to the police station and identified one young man, who, it turned out, had been living on Rikers Island for four years. My mugger associates, alas, went scot-free with my petty, petty cash. The police looked disgusted with me.

This memory has always been filled with ambivalence. I suppose one could theorize that the handshakes were meant as a form of additional humiliation, rubbing salt in the wound in my pocket. But it didn't quite feel that way. It felt more like the closing of a business meeting, neither unfriendly nor particularly amiable. The sense was of a bureaucratic commitment to form. On the one hand, I appreciated the straightforwardness of their technique—very clean—and the strangeness of their gesture has amused me to some extent. On the other hand, it smacked of a kind of professionalism that detracted from the verve they may have been seeking. I'm not trying to glibly advocate a higher aesthetic of robber brio, but there was something depressingly enigmatic about the intention of their long goodbye: the banality of decorous subway robbery?

On the train, however, it became my mission to meet my parents on time. I even saluted them with, "I hope I'm not late"—I was not—"but I was mugged by the Not-So-Merry-Men on the subway." My high-spirited affectation of nonchalance did not amuse. At the time, I clearly had problems bonding with social subgroups intent on victimizing, delayed intervening, crime solving, and waiting. All of which seems to have been rectified since I took to watching basketball on TV.

I was gifted with a new watch soon after, but I still shudder slightly when the occasional stranger asks for the time. I'm somewhat less reluctant to let it go.

THE COAT

I MADE my song a coat
Covered with embroideries
Out of old mythologies
From heel to throat

Yeats, "A Coat"

Cool Sligo, gray Sligo, promising cold and promising night. Buying a coat seemed reasonable, seemed practically sensible. Of course, I owned coats, but two were in London, where I was living, am now visiting, hanging in a hanging closet, and two were back home, gathering dust in storage. I thought, "a green raincoat with heavy lining . . . a bloated blue down . . . a triple-folded peacoat . . . a brown car coat . . ." But these thoughts did not warm me. The temperature was dropping, or my imagination was faltering, or, an ominous thought, both. A shiver was the signal of sudden determination. For years, I had trouble spending more than ten or twenty dollars at a time on clothing. I like buying clothes; I like new clothes. But years of shopping at secondhand stores had made me queasy when it came to shelling out for my shell. I remember my pleasure at my parents' horror when I would proudly announce that some shirt or sport coat they admired had cost three dollars at Goodwill. Over time, as my ventures into the once, twice, thrice used became more frequent, my pleasure in shock value turned to pride in real value. Nothing pleased me more than driving home with the new-old, thin, silk, dark-colored, appealingly worn-in tie, which cost seventy-five cents and had been overlooked for days, weeks, or years by the less discriminating or more indigent shopper. And the prospect of such pleasure in another country is multiplied, for it isn't just any bargain shirt, tie, or coat one finds, but a London shirt, a Dublin scarf, or a Sligo coat, worn originally by a cousin of Yeats, a twentieth-generation member of the gentry fallen on hard times, or a visionary, though never-published, poet. I do not despair what limbs these fabrics have touched. Nor do I dwell on the possibility of leprous old men, or young men felled by mysterious Methuselean bacteria. On that day, which could be well described as an "overcoat day," nothing could have attracted me more than a rundown second-hand shop on a side street, coats hanging in the doorway (next to a butcher shop, where other hanging shapes served up a surreal echo), that is, nothing more than a secondhand shop with no name. Nameless places tend to have a kind of prestigious mystique, a mystique summoned by the very lack of necessity for a name. In the States, we call such places the No Name Bar, or the No Name Restaurant, implying a kind of generic superiority. However, no one would have presumed to call this shop anything, not even the "No Name Place." It was too homely even for that. But the coats and the cold beckoned.

Seated behind an old high table piled with indistinct clumps of clothes, the no-name proprietor had burrowed out a hole through which he talked to an undoubtedly old friend (who shall remain nameless) and seemed surprised if not quite delighted by my presence; he treated my request for permission to try on some coats almost pleasantly, as an irrelevancy. I put on a sumptuous black cashmere coat, which made my head look like a pea. My legs and fingers, barely protruding from the sleeves, looked like dissevered doll parts; I took off the coat in record time. On the small side, I'm not unused to such discrepancies, but neither do I relish the occasional Tod Browning vision of myself in the mirror. After the first coat, the second, an indistinct pattern in a mohair blend, seemed like a gift. It seemed to fit nicely, always a surprise. But the sudden contrast lured me into fatal error: I looked into the slanted mirror on the floor and, lo, liked what I saw. The Irish, I would learn, can beguile even a wary shopper; to an experienced denizen, slanted mirrors are notorious. They can make any garment within three sizes too small or large look like it has been custom tailored. And the dim light of the shop: residents of Sligo must be well aware of tricks of the light in the land where Yeats wandered, conjuring faeries and fancies, Aengus chasing the ethereal spirit in the dim light, the witch light of the Hazelwood. I also failed to pay attention to the streaks on the mirror, preventing a clear view, dimming the contours of the coat. I bought the coat, paid the modest fifteen pounds delightedly, wore the coat for what was left of the late afternoon, the evening, and then hung it in the closet of my B and B (the weather warmed, conspiring with the mirror, with the light) until I returned to Dublin two days later on my way back to London. My conspiracy theory is abetted by the way the mistress of my Sligo lodging responded to my coat; she assured me that it was "lovely." That beautiful Irish word "lovely" is as dangerous as a slanted mirror. I was callow; I was unaware. I did not know that "lovely" is frequently a nonresponse, a neutral response. The Irish can respond with one "lovely" or with several in a row to news of fine weather, plans for the future, funeral arrangements, terrors, pleasures, the purchase of a new coat. . . . I've come to adopt it myself. Lovely.

Cold Dublin, gray with no shadings. A cold fog hung over it; life seemed impossible. I donned my Sligo coat at Connelly Station, checked my bag but kept my burgeoning pack, and ventured out for a long final tour of the city; I had eight hours to kill before the bus was to leave the train station for the ferry to Holyhead and the train to London. Though dreary, the city was not as cold as it looked. My shirt–sweater–sport coat–Sligo coat combination, along with the fifteen pounds on my back, made the time run in beads of sweat. My back began to ache. A mile or so from the station, I realized the pack would never do. I trudged back to the station, looking like an Irish Quasimodo with a green monkey on his back. They checked my burden, and the relief was immense, but the ache would not oblige by staying behind as well. I returned to the National Gallery for another viewing of the Jack Yeats and Emile Nolde watercolors; I bore the impossible crowd at its satisfying restaurant and settled for a seat in the courtyard, dining quickly in a brisk wind, which would have been impossible without my coat, I smugly thought. I then walked south to Stephen's Green, Dublin's central park, a charming little St. James.

Walking past a shop window, though, I caught a glimpse that caused me to shudder: a fleeting image of myself as a dumpy man in a frumpy coat. Trick of the light, I thought; the coat looked fine in Sligo.

I sat on a bench in the central circle of the green. The soft light of the afternoon subdued the overripe leaves into pastel. Few people out. Still life. No chill, but a perfect cool. I felt unusually calm. But reveries, spells, are made to be broken. Mine was punctured by an old man who sidled up to me on the bench. Face, a sagging mass of wrinkles leading to a smooth double chin, breathing laboriously and wearing a formless green corduroy coat and lavender pants, he edged closer to me until he was a fraction of a coat length away. He stretched his hand out and I bolted.

My wool gathering was disrupted. But I tried to wander happily, if sluggishly, through what was left of my time. Before I had to leave Dublin. Still, the disturbing image I had glimpsed an hour earlier started appearing with an alarming, a confirming frequency. I took off the coat and examined it; it looked fine, the same handsome blend I had bought. Yes, it was a coat removed from its native environs. But a changeling coat? I dismissed the idea as quickly as I had handed over fifteen pounds. I found myself on the west side of central Dublin. Secondhand clothing stores started materializing out of the encroaching darkness and mist. I walked into one aptly and almost elegantly called Second Hand, which offered a cornucopia of tweed jackets in small sizes. It also had a mirror, clean and vertically hung, in which a small man wearing a woolen tent stood with a look of desperation. Lo, he was unlovely.

I was seized with the urge to get rid of what had once been a find, something to take home. One needs to take home something, even if it's tweed. I offered to trade my fifteen-pound coat for a nine-pound jacket—"even up," as we used to say in Brooklyn. The cashier genially shook his head. I thought he looked a bit mad, but then that's how I was starting to feel. I offered the coat and three pounds (furrows on the brow of the freak in the mirror started pulsing nervously). He explained that in the absence of the proprietor he could make no deals. I pleaded; he apologized. I left. I tried an outdoor stall down the road. It was owned by the same absentee clothes merchant. She evidently inspired great fear in her employees (perhaps some Scrooge-Shylock combination, feminized with a Madame DeFarge glint in her eye), since my offer of the coat for a vest and two ties was also summarily refused. Time was running down. I felt the danger of missing the first domino of the journey back to my transient home. If I missed the bus, my first connection, I would have to fall back on the night in Dublin, for which I was eminently unprepared financially. I hated my coat more than I had ever disliked a piece of clothing. I wanted to fight my coat.

I tried one more shop: Rose's (secondhand implied). Their specialty was clearly coats; they had a dazzling array. There was a floor mirror, but it was standing upright. A middle-aged man with a sagging face full of flagging hope glared out of it from an unlovely wonderland. I tried on a black cashmere coat: too long. Then a salt-and-pepper wool and acrylic coat: the sleeves would have hit China if they hadn't been stopped by the linoleum floor. On the third try came luck, buyer's kismet: a blue calf-length coat of coarse material and perfect sleeves. It hung loosely, but fashionably, like a cape. It cost seventeen pounds. The figure in the mirror, a dashing modern highwayman, turned to the man at the cash register: "I'll give you twelve pounds and this ——"

Thirty minutes ago I was about to type the word "coat." I looked up from my desk and saw a child on bicycle slammed into by a mail truck. He or she flew fifteen, maybe twenty feet. He or she started spinning around, shrieking in pain, a wounded banshee. I ran out. There were already half a dozen people there. Two boys were running to the newsagent to call for help, running with commitment and care in their speed. I didn't need to get closer, did not need to look at a broken child. I have the twisted little thing firmly in mind. The ambulance just arrived. The crowd is larger, flashing blue lights. The familiar European siren sound changes its pitch as it approaches.

I wonder about writing this, if whoever reads it will feel tricked, annoyed by the intrusion. I wonder if I should just say "coat." I didn't have much more to say. I left the store with two coats. I was going to say that no self-respecting person should be caught dead with two coats, that that made me more self-conscious than before, that a couple of women smiled broadly at me on my way back to Connelly Station and at first I felt my sense of attractiveness regenerate, followed by the frightening possibility that they were laughing with the divined knowledge that my new coat was worse than the old coat, which pulled me up short. I was going to say (the ambulance has gone, and there is only a police car with smaller flashing lights) that I was determined to rid myself of that albatross of a coat, that I wanted to give it to a beggar, a busker, in a saintly gesture, a convenient self-apotheosis, but I didn't see any, a feat in Dublin. I left the coat hanging in a toilet stall in Connelly Station. And though I'm sure some poor unknowing soul has claimed it, not knowing what he was getting into, I think of it there, a desultory image. I was going to comment about my vanity.

Some men are pointing to the spot where the child landed. It is very close to the Chalk Farm tube station, and I'm hoping there will not be an outline in chalk. How heavy that coincidence would seem. But things come together that way sometimes; they clash, they collide, creating new, sometimes terrible, intersections. This intrusion wasn't my intention. I may have ruined the rhythm of a story, but right now I don't care. Can you understand? Nor do I have anything else to say, except that the street has resumed its normal, sullen flux.

OSTENSIBLE OCCASIONS

OCCASIONAL DESIRE

ON THE ESSAY AND THE MEMOIR

1. Memory and Desire: On Some Verses of Eliot

The allusion in my subtitle is obviously to *The Waste Land*, and less obviously to Montaigne, whose "On Some Verses of Virgil" is one of the great demonstrations of the possibility of the essay.

> April is the cruelest month, breeding
> Lilacs out of the dead land, mixing
> Memory and desire

Familiar lines, of course. But why am I invoking them here; what do I want to claim they say now? Among other things, April is the cruelest month because, as a time of transition, it stirs memory in with the desire that is emerging—memories of, perhaps, other desires, older ones. This season, spring, personified in the form of a month (April, a girl's name), is a kind of demiurge, which creates confusion because it throws us back, in the direction of memory, at the same time as we are thawing forward—such is desire. Mixing desire in with memory would make no sense in April, after winter covered earth "with forgetful snow." Spring is not the season of budding contemplation. Perhaps if December were the cruelest month, killing lilacs in a living land, desire might mix with memory, still alive but headed for a deep freeze, in a stirring cruelty, taking us from meditation to craving.

Spring is profane—as is desire.

And we might consider December, winter, sacred in its depths of spiritual or inner consideration. We might, but Eliot doesn't, not in "The Burial of the Dead," where the sacred had languished into corruption.

Still, does Eliot mean, to extend, to schematically extrapolate the metaphor, that memory is sacred?

Well, memory might be sacred, which is to say that one experiences it as such. Anything might be. In *The Waste Land* we plunge into parodic nostalgic recollection—a half-sweet, half-curdled memory of youthful winter pleasures, when Europe seemed whole, before the land was wasted, was laid waste to. Wholeness, we know, and the reclamation of European culture, and of course that inscrutably benevolent monarch God, would increasingly fill Eliot's desires, which mixed with his memory, reversing the equation I suggested above. In *Four Quartets*, desire seems mixed with memory in an ultimately painful ecstasy: "There is only the fight to recover what has been lost / And found and lost again and again." Then, in the last stanza, "We shall not cease from exploration / And the end of all our exploring / Will be to arrive where we started / And know the place for the first time." Desire for the transcendent knowledge of God will take Eliot back . . . with perception utterly changed, changed utterly. His desire makes memory dynamic.

All of this is to suggest that memory and desire swirl around each other, or take turns riding one another, or perhaps they're symbiotic, parasite and host exchanging places as time allows or demands. Luckily, metaphors for memory and desire are inexhaustible, (see David Lowenthal's *The Past Is a Foreign Country* or *Metaphors of Memory* by Souwe Draaisma) or we'd all be in a pretty pickle, a pinch, a box. But my real question, in case you doubted I had one, is, how do we and how might we think of the relationship of memory and desire with regard to autobiographical writing, more specifically autobiographical prose?

What kind of bedfellows can memory and desire be? How is memory colored by desire? How does desire inflect and infect memory? How do they joust or caress, repel or require one another?

To this I have a simple answer: I'd love to remember if I ever knew, but since I don't, I'm forced to believe that the answer is escapable. In other words, thinking I know that this relationship is too complex to unravel or solve, I have to resist simplification, forced resolution, merely incidental connection, and glib disentanglements. In other words, I have to approach the subject as I approach most others: as an essayist; my desire to understand this subject and any invocation of the past should be instruments that I use warily and strategically. Let me cut to the chase (a phrase I remember fondly from my days in Brooklyn school yards—*Marie, hold on tight?*): when we are in memory mode, when we remember, we almost always have an ulterior motive, even when we have an anterior one. I remember my mother on a day, let's say in spring, in 1963, when I was six (and April wasn't cruel). Why? Why do I perform this memory? How do I perform this memory? Do I engage in a process of duplication, trying to re-create a memory I've envisaged before? Or am I approaching it differently this time, circling around her from the left instead of the right as she sits on the stoop and smokes? Is her housedress plaid, hemline right at the center of the knee (*Do I dare to eat a peach?*)? Or is she dressed in the vague halos, the fogs of memory that fill in the details we aren't focusing on? Is the memory static or a mnemonic changeling, a shape-shifting child of Mnemosyne, mother of the Muses? Here I'm thrown back to Henri Bergson (is my memory thawing or cooling into intellection?), a significant influence on Eliot coincidentally enough (is it?). Bergson speaks of mechanical time and dulled senses, the object we vaguely see but do not go past the familiarity of, do not vitally register. When we're in this sensually dulled-out state, we're far from what he called the "*élan vital*," which in Bergson's description sounds like a fugue state with a view. To simplify: too often we treat memory blandly and with a kind of willfully perverse reification. This makes for autobiographical writing that pays homage to unexamined lives, our own and others'.

Why do I want to remember my mother in 1963? This is the, in a chronological accident (is it an accident?), $64,000 question. Is it because in missing the long dead, one salves one's wounds through re-creation? Or am I rubbing a wound, seeing how much it hurts, or whether it does? Why did I just change pronouns, from the personal "I" to the impersonal "one." And why the change back again? Is there something I need to know about my mother? About my mother in 1963? About me in 1963? About my mother and me in 1963? Or is the question, like dream work, off to the side, hiding behind the couch, in the broom closet, in my repressed desire or my self-conscious but incomplete desire? In short, what do I want? And an important distinction for me: am I invoking a memory, a simulacrum of what happened that I have thought of as static or performing a more active act of remembering, holding it, the memory, in my hands (*Marie, hold on tight*) and turning it around, upside down?

Generically, this question, for me, speaks profoundly to the differences in kinds of autobiographical writing, most intensely, but not exclusively, the difference between the essay and the memoir.

Some further complications: Many of the memoirs being published today are what might be called collections of autobiographical essays that are more or less chronological. I'd love to say what the essay collections being published today are, but there are so few of them that I can't . . . There are many collections called books of essays—essays lite, I call them—but many of these lack the tension, the structural and organizational complexity, and a resistance to the pleasantries and facilities of the genial personal essay voice that give the genre its credibility. These may be anything from self-help books (psycho–babbling brooks of watery promise) to autobiographical excursions that insist on epiphany to collections of columns or reviews that are like essays in short pants (or kneesocks); they seem to have never quite grown up. Among the latter, I'd list, and please groan on cue in shocked disapproval, Dave Barry, a writer whose insistent triviality makes me more than slightly dyspeptic, and Anna Quindlen, who seemed to speak for a generation of urban women, until she herself seemed to tire of her generic representativeness and turned to novels, only to turn again to essays with, are you ready, *Lots of Candles, Plenty of Cake*—do I need to start celebrating before I even start reading? On the literary side, Annie Dillard, a talented writer whose gifts seem squandered, is too insistently spent, in books like *For the Time Being*, in constant and consistent lyricism and gelatinous thinking. Or Carl Hiaasen—one gear. These are writers lacking sufficient friction, or tension—one of the essentials of good literary art. (Yes, I said good. We say it constantly but wince when writing it. And why must so much of criticism by writers take the low roads of the stinging ad hominem or indiscriminate praise? Montaigne, anyone?) You may have guessed by now that I'm more a denizen of solitary confinement than a seeker of writerly solidarity. Montaigne said in "On Some Verses of Virgil" that that essay would get his work placed in the boudoir: too honest, too scandalous, too close to the bone. Too many writers merely want their work placed. As an aside, I think wanting to be a writer is a perfectly charming reason for wanting to write, at first. But if it doesn't fall away like a chrysalis, it becomes a kind of grotesque atavism. Wanting to write about or from or toward is always more promising than merely wanting to write. It makes me cringe when I hear people say this. And there are well-established writers who seem to have never quite caught on, producing book after book on the dreary road to a body of work. Someone please make Frances Mayes promise to stop publishing books for at least five years or, à la George Perec, not use the letter "t." I like writers of limited original output, like James Agee or Philip Larkin, Robert Burton or Elizabeth Smart, Jacques Roubaud . . . But I digress . . .

The autobiographical essay, the personal essay proper, whose lineage is Hazlittian, Lambian, Woolfian, usually contains or contrasts memory and desire, producing resistance through friction: this is what I'd like to believe, and this is what I think is true, albeit contingently. There is a profound difference between Nancy Mairs or Richard Rodriguez or Edward Hoagland or Vivian Gornick and the light essay or short piece of memoir (we need a term for such work: memoirette? autobiografillies? memory prose?). And the difference comes down (rises?) to the centrality of ideas.

The memoir, in long or short form, is usually content heavy, narratively driven, and, in the American literary marketplace today, dependent on a "hook": substance abuse, physical abuse, strange adventures, exotic backgrounds, any aspect of what Nancy Mairs has called "the literature of personal disaster." The memoir piece frequently sees a memory as sacred, immutable, or transcendent, mistily mysterious even if seemingly understandable. I frequently teach Kathryn Harrison's *The Kiss* as an example of how a book can have outstanding literary qualities and still be a disaster nonfictionally. *The Kiss* makes me want to scream (Rodin meets Munch in a battle of dubbed Japanese superartists?). Of course, if a memoir were to question every moment it rendered, it would be bogged down in infinite regressions, as the narrator of John Barth's *Floating Opera* suggests: to write my autobiography, I must write my father's, and so on . . . On the other hand, in not questioning enough, the memoir risks nostalgia, or whitewashing, or a kind of fictional re-creation that may have more to do with . . . some desires (e.g., to re-create, to publish, to burnish, to enshrine) than others (e.g., to demystify, to consider, to enlarge one's subject, to self-investigate). The memoir frequently performs memory for its audience of voyeurs, who vicariously enter the narrative. The memoir wants to entertain us, the reader—it needs, craves our interest. As such, it can be a bit whorish. And you thought the sentimental whore died with Camille? The memoir's occasion is frequently quite simple: this is a good story to tell, with lively characters given a vervy charge by having actually existed. It may record, valuably, a period of time, a place, a place in time. Memoirists are usually lyrical—after all, heaven knows they've got time.

The essay, in contrast, is voice driven, question filled, metaphysically complex. Ultimately, its questions always threaten to overwhelm any possible answers. Not "this is what happened," but "what happened, and what did it mean, and why am I remembering it, and what does that say about me?" The essay leans toward the profane, toward a severe attitude concerning memory. It mixes memory and desire and tries to separate them, to disinfect the effects of fearful or dubious desires. It desires to understand its desire. It threatens to sink the narrative ship, to send chronology rolling away down a steep hill, while it stops and argues with itself. The essayist accepts the reader looking over her shoulder or may enlist the reader as an accomplice, an intimate, in the process of self-examination, in the processes of asking difficult questions of any subject it turns to. But in its classic form, the essay doesn't quite know where the hell it's going to go from the outset. The essay's occasion, an implicit or explicit question, is a grain of sand disturbing the oyster, the writer's complacency in whatever form it may have taken or be taking. If essayists sometimes sound querulous, it is because they frequently have a rock in their shoe. Or the essayist may at times seem a bit manic, digressing in a flailing way, as a way of trying to get somewhere, anywhere. Joseph Epstein, an essayist who I am convinced was a curmudgeonly child, has written a book of essays called *At the End of My Tether*.

One generic difficulty in contrasting the contemporary essay to the short memoir is that the essay as practiced and taught in creative writing programs seems to me too dominated by autobiography. The idea of using a personal voice to discuss a subject—whether it's Schubert or baseball or, dare we speak the name, an idea, say that good old Montaignian chestnut "Friendship" or "The Disadvantages of Intellectual Superiority" or a new *Three Guineas* of our current sense of war—seems remote from the sense of the essay. An admission: I don't have much to go on for evidence here other than what I see under "essays" in literary magazines, what is sent to me as an editor, and what my students have read at other programs before coming to study at Ohio University. Susan Sontag, Robert Nozick, Alphonso Lingis, Hannah Arendt, Martha Nussbaum, Andrea Dworkin, Susan Griffin, Cynthia Ozick . . . these are precisely the kinds of essayists that my students haven't read. Let me overload my case while I'm at it: Carlyle, Pater, Stendhal, Anatole France, Max Beerbohm, all seem to have drifted away from many of the current practitioners of the form as possible models. I confess there are days when I can barely respond to the overwhelming sameness of autobiographical tastes many students bring from their essay reading: David Sedaris, Annie Dillard, David Sedaris, David Sedaris, David Sedaris. And I've certainly been guilty of writing my share of autobiographical essays (*j'accuses* should begin at home), though I've also inflicted on readers essays on film and photography and painting. I'm not arguing that essayists should not use or write their experiences, but that there is a world of ideas out there worth thinking about on the page. I think, I sense, that many writers, especially young writers, venturing into the essay form have been raised on the autobiographical essay rather too exclusively. This is to say they don't have a thorough education in the form. Why be polite. Many writers of autobiographical essays couldn't tell a Montaigne from a Bacon, a Browne from a Donne, a Hellman from a McCarthy. But they can remember lyrically and ruefully. They can evoke. And they are both drawn to and frequently have been placed on a diet that may not be quite balanced enough for their long-term best interests as writers. This may be another way of saying that I fear the essay is being democratized out of urgency and potency, out of its many possibilities, something like what happened to poetry in the 1970s and 1980s: more writers, fewer committed readers. There are a lot of essays out there, but it seems as though they're much of a kind, a subgenre dominating and representing the genre for potential writing neophytes, for other readers who aren't as interested in the testy, testing, complex history of the essay.

This is why I'm so fiercely fond of Rachel Blau DuPlessis's work on the essay, in *The Pink Guitar* and her essay "f-Words: An Essay on the Essay." While DuPlessis is much more displeased than I at the very thought of autobiographical writing, in the narrative sense, her work is a corrective, a tonic, to the sloppy thought and easy lyricism that passes for essays these days. How can anyone, I wonder, not trust enough to listen to a writer who says the following:

> But if essays are works of "reading," they are also works "wrought," a thinking that occurs through the material fabrication of language, a work and a working in language, not simply a working through intellectually or emotionally—language not as a summary of findings but as the inventor of findings. Wrought is the past participle of work, but I had always thought (wrongly, but willfully) that wreaking was a related word. Reading and wreaking make a euphonious pair. However, wreaking in its real meaning is at the extreme end of the essay—its wrath, its venting of anger, its drive. But I think if a wreaking could be sweetened just somewhat—its propulsions made positive instead of vengeful—one would have the sense of the energy of the essay, its wayward reach into utopic desires.

Clearly, anything is possible within the fugitive reader, as well as the fugitive writer. But DuPlessis reminds us that essays that are lamely belletristic, that are "too nice," are probably not using the form actively enough (E. B. White, hold on tight). And stirringly, she also makes the case for the essay's adoption as a form of *feminine ecriture* (in the largest sense), that in its avoidance of linear movement, conventional wisdom, and complacencies of the pen, it has always had the qualities of an "excessive writing practice," "forever skeptical, forever alert, forever yearning" ("f-words). (Rachel, here's my list of essay descriptions, fond as I am of *d*'s: desire, disruption, discovery, dyspepsia, disturbing, disturbed, distemper, dissonant, disquietude, disgraceful, discursive, discomfiture, dereliction, Daedalian, doubt, DuPlessian . . .)

I've discussed the memoirization of the essay, but there are certainly cases of the essayification of the memoir or autobiography. Nathalie Sarraute understood the essay mode beautifully in her autobiographical *Childhood* (*Enfances*). She divides herself into two voices (it could be ten, of course, or one with more integrated selves). One voice is the lyrical voice of memory: it is filled with desire—it wants things to have turned out all right. The second voice, profane, is slightly demonic or daemonic, pushing the first voice around, questioning her interpretations, impatient with the beautification of memory, the beatification of memory. It provides resistance, driving a necessary wedge between memory and desire.

Listen to these two in one, this one in two voices with "it," Sarraute's object and ostensible subject, her childhood:

—That's just it: what I'm afraid of, this time, is that it isn't trembling . . . not enough . . . that it has become fixed once and for all, "a sure thing," decided in advance . . .

—Don't worry about it having been decided in advance . . . it's still vacillating, no written word, no word of any sort has yet touched it, I think it is still faintly quivering . . . outside words . . . as usual . . . little bits of something still alive . . . I would like . . . before they disappear . . . let me . . .

—Right. I won't say any more . . . and in any case, we know very well that when something starts haunting you . . .

—Yes, and this time, it's hardly believable, but it was you who prompted me, for some time now you have been inciting me . . .

—I?

—Yes, you, by your admonitions, your warnings . . . you conjure it up, you immerse me in it . . .

What emerges is a meditation on memory, a theory of memory as necessarily incomplete. And this is where Sarraute (along with Georges Perec and Michel Leiris and Christa Wolf and Susan Griffin . . .) differs from most contemporary memoirists: not just the thing itself (memory), but ideas about the thing, a process more common to the essay than to conventional autobiography.

My mother's housedress must sit in the closet. I'm afraid it isn't germane to this essay, no matter how much it might be to something else, anything else, I might write. Avoidance, led by the leash of decorum, can be exemplary, or at least A-OK.

This essay is marked by some modernist allusions; like most writers who are interested in the postmodern—as in the incomplete, the contingent, the fragmentary, unresolved and unsystematized—I'm really a late modernist at heart. And I feel that the essay, rather than the narrative memoir (memoiritty? memza?), best suits my interests, my intellectual and emotional temperament. Narrative without resistance, memory and desire unacknowledged as cohorts, tries to use wholeness to shore against its fragments. That ruins things for me; I just can't buy it.

The best essay's sheets are rumpled, askew; it sits on the corner of the bed with one eyebrow raised. Memoir, too often, stands at the window in white linen; it gazes out wistfully, not admitting it wants a large greasy breakfast.

II. *On the Occasional*

Nothing seems to me more central than the idea and execution of the occasion of an autobiographical work. But the occasion has a different function depending on the kind of book one is writing. As I mention in the essay, the occasion of an autobiographical work may be rather simple, even when the book itself is complex. Of course, the book may also be equally simple.

For example, in *Riding in Cars with Boys* the occasion is Beverly Donofrio taking her son to college, wondering how she could have raised such a normal child. Her last twenty years, therefore, don't quite jive with her first twenty, and she's going to tell us why.

In *Truth*, by Ellen Douglas, the occasion is in the subtitle: *Four Stories I Am Finally Old Enough to Tell*. The implication is clear—her memories, some of her memories, are painful or shocking, family revelations that may have felt like betrayals at an earlier stage in life. Here, by the by, we might remember Joan Didion's warning at the beginning of *Slouching towards Bethlehem* that writers are always selling somebody out. The occasion that reveals family secrets always sells the family out, no matter how justified, necessary, or balanced.

Treetops, by Susan Cheever, has a split occasion: The genially general memoir occasion of capturing a time and place, the eponymous treetops. And she tells us that, after writing *Home before Dark*, "I began to see that I had told only half the story—my father's story. The myths he created about himself were part of a larger family legacy: a history passed on and embroidered to serve its members." So, occasion two is the desire for balance, an occasion that is self-generated, since the world in all likelihood does not register that only half a story has been told. And here I must digress to discuss this intermingling of public and private motive. Certainly one's memories performed, rehashed, explored in writing always entail this mix. But I always find it interesting and curious when the writer asserts that the record needed to be set straight. Of course it didn't. As readers, we couldn't care less about the imbalance of revealed family history, unless of course it reads as imbalanced, as skewed or self-deceiving or protectively partial. My students always ask, naturally enough, the truth question about writing nonfiction. How true must one be, should one be, can one be . . . What if we decided to lie and completely revised the ending of an autobiographical narrative? My answer to them is complex: no one would probably know, though your own process would be utterly compromised and might not lead you to the most important nonfictive places you're capable of reaching. The most important part of nonfiction isn't about fact—it's about what experience means. That's why overtly manipulating facts has never made much sense to me. This doesn't mean works that confound their factual sources lack admirable or important literary qualities. I just don't understand why they bother.

And perhaps this is where we need to meditate on the case of Lillian Hellman. In 1971 Mary McCarthy was on the Dick Cavett show and was opining on the relative merits of American writers who were "overrated." To be fair, she was asked the question, and in retrospect it seems something of a set-up, though also to be fair (and here I lean the other way like a tottering ship), one must point out that McCarthy was no neophyte lured into error by a worldlier interviewer. She took the bait, when Cavett asked her about Lillian Hellman. Now, Hellman and McCarthy—the twin doyennes of the New York literary world, approximate contemporaries in their sixties—represented the unreconstructed left (Hellman) and the liberal anticommunist brigade (McCarthy). In other words, they were the Cain and Abel of political siblings. What about Lillian Hellman? McCarthy replied, "Every word she's ever written is a lie, including 'and,' and 'the.'" The next day in New York Civil Court, Hellman sued McCarthy for slander, a suit that would drag on and only reach its final conclusion when Hellman died. What happened in the interim, however, was a consequential attention given to the autobiographical prose works that Hellman had been writing to great acclaim: *An Unfinished Woman, Scoundrel Time* (in which Hellman talks of her experience with another McCarthy, Joseph, who sent her emphysemic partner, Dashiell Hammett, to prison, and prompting Hellman to write to the committee, when they requested that she testify, a line that should be infamous: "I will not cut my conscience to fit this year's fashions"). Alas, it would seem that some years later Hellman did. The middle essay of her third collection, *Pentimento*, the central essay in fact, is called "Julia," which was made into a film starring Jane Fonda and Vanessa Redgrave, directed by Fred Zinneman. It is movingly middlebrow stuff, and the only essay I can think of to be turned into a film, though I think Chaplin was contemplating "The Death of the Moth" by Virginia Woolf. Seriously, though, the essay is about serious stuff: Hellman smuggles money into Berlin in the early forties so her lifelong friend, almost inamorata, can help save Jews, Catholics, and others in peril. The mission is a success, but Julia, Vanessa Redgrave, begins to languish, is imprisoned . . . Hellman returns and eventually, in the afterglow of her career, writes this concentrated, moving, amazing chronicle. Amazingly moving. Movingly amazing. Never happened.

No need for a readerly double take. Hellman essentially made the whole thing up, including the woman formerly known as

Julia, who was based on an actual person whom Hellman may have known most fleetingly. And the lawsuit was the *machina* that set the discovery in motion. To which we might ask:

Is the book now sold as fiction? No.

Did Hellman ever admit the fabrications? No. (And note the force of nonfictive gullibility among readers: why did anyone believe that a Jewish American playwright went on a covert mission to Berlin in the early 1940s?)

Do we know less about Hellman as a consequence? No, ironically, we know more, since we know how she would, how she did construct a narrative so propelled by her desire—that word again—that she, in writing, lived the lie, performed a preferred life. Along with much other material whose veracity is unquestioned or untested.

What is the occasion of a narrative that never happened? For our purposes, I would say this were the $64,000 question if (*a*) that, too, hadn't been a hoax and (*b*) anyone cared to pay that much for the *corpus delecti* of an essay—again, desire to be other than who one is.

Most of us, though, are simply not important enough for anyone to bother to check on our facts. In any case, no matter what the kind of literary nonfiction, the facts are never the primary importance of the work. Facts are self-sufficient. They don't need literature. It is the interpretation of fact that all literary nonfiction is based on. Here I might remind you of Phillip Roth's autobiographical *The Facts*. After a rather quick and listless recitation of his memory's salient moments, Roth's book is critiqued in an afterward by his autobiographical character Zuckerman. Problem is that Zuckerman is, in my opinion, quite right about the defects of the book, and the cleverness of imitative form is never sufficient. We don't want to read a bad performance for the comedy of the critique. In *Operation Shylock*,

Roth, with the occasion of recovery from Halcion-induced mania, performs a much defter dance on the borderlines of fiction and nonfiction, that region where the literary pale begins.

Back to occasions: much more convincing than "because it was" or "because I am," as an excuse for autobiographical excursions, is "because I am because it was." Or he, she, or they. The author has reached a point in life where difficult questions can be asked, where the self is complicated enough in adult history and knowledge of the world (including literary knowledge) to be able to undertake an exploration. This is similar to Ellen Douglas's *Truth*, but perhaps less delayed, less an endgame. One can, or one must, summon the past, to put ghosts to rest, or to raise the restless spirits, or both. Edward Dahlberg, at the beginning of *Because I Was Flesh*, writes, "Kansas City was the city of my youth, and the burial ground of my poor mother's hopes; her blood, like Abel's, cries out to me from every cobblestone, building, flat and street." There is no way of predicting, until the end of this most oedipal of narratives, that Dahlberg will arrive at the deliriously excessive lyricism of his final invocation: "and when I regard her wild tatters, I know that not even Solomon in his lilied raiment was so glorious as my mother in her rags." Apologies, but Frank McCourt, please step aside; the title of *Angela's Ashes* predicts exactly where the memoir will go, and the portrait of Angela seems relatively static to me.

Occasions are, of course, limitless. But there are classics that recur: I must tell this story, to (*a*) try to find out what really happened, (*b*) try to find out what it meant, (*c*) make sure that an important element of our culture is not forgotten, (*d*) exorcise the demons that sit on the edge of these experiences like fallen angels, (*e*) represent a set of experiences that has never been captured. This last has, of course, fueled the rise of memoir in the United States over the last thirty years, as memoirs by women, African Americans, Latin Americans, Asian Americans, the LGBT community . . . flock to shelves that had once been closed to them, like restricted country clubs. There they join the memoirs of personal disaster I alluded to above, which has also been in short supply thanks to cultural ignorance, or censorship of the Puritan or Victorian or more vaguely squeamish variety.

But I want to stress again that essay almost always leads with a stronger occasion than autobiography, so if you're thinking of writing an autobiographical work, your leading question should be, why? If it's to share what you consider an interesting story, you had best be a master storyteller. If it's to discover what your story is, you'd better be willing to ask the difficult questions and accept the difficult answers, if any come knocking.

But to reiterate, or perhaps to iterate, your occasion is an act of deference of sorts. I am here telling you about myself for a reason. And the reason is . . . Even if the reason is "I need to try to find out what the reason is."

An occasion may, of course, be complex and multiple. For example, my students at Ohio University working on the essay were hard-pressed to not write about the destruction of the World Trade Center in Manhattan. What's the occasion? A laughable question, ostensibly. We were citizens of a country in crisis, an Orwellian wet dream of the occasional (pardon the gender specificity), but dangerous in its obviousness, the grandeur, the greatness of its tragic inherency. I say dangerous because it is difficult for any essayist to invoke tragedy; it's not essentially a tragic form. In any case, why the specific writer? We know what might bring anyone to want to write about this subject, but what brings this writer to the occasion? If I were writing it, the secondary—in this case, personal occasion—would suggest itself easily. My family used to dine frequently at Windows on the

World, the restaurant at the top of the center. I remember one Christmas, my brother's birthday, watching the snow fall and gradually cover the city, my city, now so distantly, so gradually indistinctly, below me. A very different covering, a more innocent veil, than the one of two weeks ago. Or I might have something to say about the towers being completed when I was thirteen, when my lower Manhattan started vying with my upper Manhattan for dominance. It's the Manhattan project of pubescence, or something of the sort.

And my students from Sandusky or Youngstown, Chicago or Normal, what's their personal occasion, if they aren't gifted with the political insight or rhetorical gifts of a Nat Hentoff or Ellen Willis, a Christopher Hitchens, not to mention Baldwin or Orwell? It might be a consideration far from the epicenter of media and culture in our country. Seeing the second plane slam into tower two on a TV screen in the student center or their disaster of an apartment could set off a wonderful chain of essaying about language—disaster, let's say, or center—or a mediation on how that student was driven inward, away from the body politic, by the mass media's hype about war, which she has never had the opportunity to experience fully as a member of the American polity . . . The personal is rarely at odds with the political, is so, in fact, only as a statement of extreme alienation, which is in itself a potentially useful, informative, chilling, or heartbreaking statement on the state of our culture in microcosm or a certain part of it. And my teasing of Orwell is born of—let's avoid the very un-Orwellian idolatry—let's say, the deepest writerly respect.

It is for this reason that on the evening of September 11, 2001, in teaching my shocked class for fifteen minutes or so, I read them the following snippets from Orwell, this first from his essay "England Your England":

As I write, highly civilized human beings are flying over-head, trying to kill me. They do not feel any enmity against me as an individual, nor I against them. They are "only do-ing their duty," as the saying goes. Most of them, I have no doubt, are kind-hearted law-abiding men who would nev-er dream of committing murder in private life. On the oth-er hand, if one of them succeeds in blowing me to pieces with a well-placed bomb, he will never sleep any the worse for it. He is serving his country, which has the power to ab-solve him from evil. One cannot see the modern world as it is unless one recognizes the overwhelming strength of patriotism, national loyalty. In certain circumstances it can break down, at certain levels of civilization it does not ex-ist, but as a positive force there is nothing to set beside it. Christianity and international socialism are as weak as straw in comparison with it. Hitler and Mussolini rose to power in their own countries very largely because they could grasp this fact and their opponents could not.

Applying Orwell to our current situation, we might speculate that the force of Islamic terrorism in the world is fueled by re-ligion experienced as nationalism, nationalism with the spiri-tual dimension of religion—an inordinately powerful and ter-rifying combination. To move on, though, Orwell extends his consideration to the idea that there really are considerable dif-ferences in people from culture to culture, an idea that seems both contrary to certain kinds of humanistic sentimentality, and self-evident. Orwell writes,

In fact anyone able to use his eyes knows that the average of human behavior differs enormously from country to coun-try. Things that could happen in one country could not happen in another. Hitler's June Purge, for instance, could not have happened in England.

Just so, and despite my most cynical liberal bona fides, I didn't feel that the Bush administration, name notwithstanding, was going to be checking beard lengths. Orwell then moves, naturally enough, to a discussion of what makes the English different, arriving first at the feeling that "When you come back to England from any foreign country, you have immediately the sensation of breathing a different air." What follows is typical Orwell—memorable images that embody characteristics and ideology and progressive countermyths masquerading as unbiased analysis, utterly convincing along the way. But to return to my larger subject, which is to say the one I began with, Orwell moves from his immediate occasion in the moment of writing, in real if mitigated danger (the chance of a bomb landing on him is possible, though unlikely), to a more general sense of who hypothetical victim and perpetrator are, to the national differences of countries generally, to his analysis of what makes the English who they are, the relationship of character and characteristic. The occasion is that a way of life is at stake: morally complex and frequently stupid, slow to change with more hurried change on the horizon, classist, devoted to the domestic pleasure of gardening. The occasion has moved from what might happen to me to what might happen to us.

As you may have noticed, I have moved from autobiography and memoir to the essay. Surprised? Am I not performing my own desire in this essay, the occasion being, among other things, a response to autobiography's seeming hegemony in the world of "creative nonfiction." Perhaps we need a separate camp, of destructive nonfiction, a wider, wilder, grayer zone, in which the essay and other fugitive forms, known and as yet undiscovered, can ply their wayward trades, following those occasional desires into open forms that—like the figure of my mother in 1963, for me—challenge facets of the imagination beyond the complacencies of memory's narratives.

QUEERING THE ESSAY

Let me be known all at once for a queer fellow

RICHARD STEELE, *Spectator*, no. 474, p. 2

Genre and gender are indissolubly linked, etymologically intertwined. Clearly the two words emerge from an intertwined root system that speaks to typologies, distinctions, styles—and they are almost homonyms, fraternal sound twins. Turn to genre in the dictionary, and you will be pointed to gender. Early uses of *genre* cited in the *Oxford English Dictionary* refer to distinguishing types of people; the first cited, interestingly, by Lady Morgan, says, "But what is the genre of character . . . which, if in true keeping to life and manners, should not be found to resemble any body" (1818). How queer, that one of the first uses of *genre* suggests a person who is impossible to characterize. Genre is a category after all. So is gender. And the gender category difficult to characterize by normative standards is queer. The genre category difficult or impossible to characterize, the essay, is also queer. The essay is the queer genre.

The words have further etymological complexities when one considers that *gender* can be translated into *genre* in French, *genero* in Spanish, and *genere* in Italian—the Latin stem form of "genus," "kind." The Greek root of *gen* means "to produce," which gives us *genesis, oxygen, gene*.

In Leviticus, God says, "Thou shalt not let thy cattle gender with a diverse kind; thou shall not sow thy field with a mingled seed." We can imagine the result, a genre of hybrid calves or, worse yet, queer cattle mingling all over the place. They wouldn't know what to call them.

The history of genre has evolved through Western literature as a story of creating distinctions, discrete categories for the most part, and subdivision. Poetry, fiction, and drama, with their various subgeneric extensions, period demarcations, stylistic innovations: Romantic poetry, the epistolary novel, kitchen-sink drama, ad infinitum. But until now, one of our major genres, the essay, has resisted classification. Has resisted *genrification*. To read through the history of essays on the essay is, to a large and fascinating extent, to see practitioners of the form struggling to articulate what the form is and refusing to keep the form stable, refusing to narrow its sense of possible performative and formal dimensions, frequently inverting commonly accepted conventions (idling is good and natural, sensibility and self-awareness are virtues, intense attention to the self leads to an enlarged perspective, eros is located profoundly in friendship). Nancy Mairs, Rachel Blau DuPlessis, and others have suggested a feminine affinity for the essay, feminizing Montaigne along the way, which is quite a trick when one considers how excessively women are discounted in Montaigne's overt discourse. But Rachel Blau DuPlessis suggests in "f words: An Essay on the Essay" that the openness, distrust of systems, skepticism, and transgressive nature of the form are reasons "why the essay has been summed up the by the term feminine." And in "Essaying the Feminine: From Montaigne to Kristeva," Nancy Mairs finds qualities in the "Montaignesque" essay that break or escape phallocentric discourse. At the end of "On Some Verses of Virgil," Montaigne does say, shockingly, that "except for education and habit, the difference [between the sexes] is not great."

I'd go a step further, suggesting that the essay as a genre doesn't just resist classic gender binaries but, in many ways, queers them. I'll pull the statement out of the rhetorical closet: the essay *is* a queer genre. What do I mean? I mean this in a most specific way—in the way that queer theory defines *queer* as a continuing instability in gender relations that undermines the traditional binary of gender, replacing it with indeterminate, transgressive desires. The desire of the essay is to transgress genre.

Queer and *essay* are both problematic, escapable, changeable terms. Both imply resistance and transgression, definitional defiance. But there is more; for example, Judith Butler's sense of performativity and gender and performativity's importance to the constitution of gender through reiteration speak to the operation of persona in the essay. Much has been written about persona, but we know this: it is never fully controlled or calibrated; it is subversive and always has been, because, like gender performance, it "is the kind of effect that resists calculation" to at least some extent.

The most memorable essays are formally labile and so stretch our sense of what essays might be. All essays think, come to ideas, create lasting images, seem to have some association with their personae. The elasticity of persona itself is part of the essay's queerness. I mean this both in a metaphorical sense and as it speaks to gender. Look at the queerness at the heart of the essay: Woolf and Baldwin, Rodriguez and Fisher, Barthes and Lamb.

The essay is not and has never been genre normative; this is essential to the nature of the essay. Calling the essay "lyrical" or even "personal" puts a generic leash on it, domesticates it under the guise of setting the essay onto untrammelled ground. However, for 430 years the (not so) simple noun *essay* has allowed us to resist the normalizing impulses that govern other genres, and has led to Pascal and Sebald and M. F. K. Fisher. What is queer about the essay is its resistance to stability, categories—even the one I'm advancing in this essay. The best theories of the essay—by Lukacs, Adorno, Montaigne, Emerson, DuPlessis—turn in on themselves, lose argumentative coherence in the direction of passionate, expansive thinking about the essay. Essays about the essay tend to be transgressively shapely, as much as any other essay, if we think shapely and circuitous are lively and harmonious concepts, as I do.

Réda Bensmaïa, perhaps the most compelling contemporary critic of the essay, writes in *The Barthes Effect*, that

> Among all the terms that relate to the literary genres, the word Essay is certainly the one that has given rise to the most confusion in the history of literature; since Montaigne used the term to describe his writings, 'essay' has served to designate works that are so diverse from a formal point of view, and so heterogeneous from a thematic point of view, that it has become practically impossible to subsume a single, definitive type of text under this term."

Bensmaïa goes on to note, and pay attention to the language, that until recently, the genre of the essay, "A unique case in the annals of literature," "is the only literary genre to have resisted integration . . . in the taxonomy of genres." The language and connection to gender seem clear enough. The essay has been the queer genre, borrowing from, at times parodying, other forms, constantly creating new unstable ones, but never—queerly—fully taxonomized, defined, institutionally appropriated.

Perhaps until now.

John Frow speaks of genre as a form of symbolic action. If this is the case, what have essayists enacted, symbolically spoken by writing essays. What has it meant "to essay"? Has this question ever really been asked, other than formally? I would argue that to essay has frequently been a generically queer behavior, writing this form that resists and undermines other categories. It is also a form that asks for secrets to be exposed and feelings to be explored, has asked for memory to be reconsidered, and for gender roles to be stretched (think of the end of "On Some Verses of Virgil"), for outlandish, strange, unsympathetic, or merely whimsical ideas to emerge as we adapt or adopt personae and extend the reach of our empathetic imagination.

Bensmaïa argues that the essay, "born practically and aesthetically with Montaigne . . . still had to be born theoretically [unlike other genres] . . . above all with Roland Barthes, this genre judged 'unclassifiable' for a long time was finally able to make its 'theoretical entrance' into the history of literature and the theory of literary genres." As theory, the essay also retains its essence as a fragmentary book of the self. Clearly, with Barthes as the theoretical impresario, the queerness of the genre, the way it signifies its refusals, its openness, its difference, both becomes obvious and, to Bensmaïa, approaches a kind of generically canonical status. If this is true, it may ironically undermine the essay's queerness over time and also exactly explain why the taxonomy of essays is going on now. The essay, queerly, has always existed ahistorically. The development of "new" forms like the lyric essay may be an attempt to usher the essay into a more conventional evolutionary pattern, with the lyric essay as the postmodern phase of the form. The irony is that it makes the essay seem more taxonomically like other forms of literature and, therefore, less queer, less resistant to typologies, and also that it may appropriate the form into the more conventional genres, like poetry. Of course, essays have always indulged in hybridic behavior, transgendered.

Are essayists queer? Yes, or they have been, I'd argue, because along with the great motto of the essay, Montaigne's "Que sais-je" (which carries with it the duality of inflection: what do *I* know, and what I *know*), I've always thought the other great line that spoke to the heart of the essay—and perhaps I'm giving myself away as an essayist, but I believe this is reflected in the prismatically digressive attentiveness of the essay voice—comes in fiction, in Henry James's *The Art of Fiction*, when he urges us to "Try and be one of the people on whom nothing is lost." Essays embody sensibility and a sense of self (think of Hazlitt's "On Gusto") and the feeling, embodied in style, of the essayist's difference from everyone else, even when speaking of common things. I wish James had written expansive essays, in addition to the prefaces of the New York edition. In his famous letter to Henry Adams, he writes, "I am that queer monster, an obstinate finality, an inexhaustible sensibility."

Perhaps there is an element of queer desire in this very subject for me, my desire to be a queer essayist, marking my sense of the genre itself, spilling over, if you will. But perhaps again this is my point itself. I want to betray my motives, want my sensibility to color the world I'm seeing, and the literary world I inhabit, and I want to lose nothing in trying to be aware of how this coloration is taking shape, even in its potential excessiveness.

In the case of Charles Lamb, we see an extreme version of the essay's queerness most vividly, as Lamb, struggling with the intensity of his discourse, the sensibility of self-protective nostalgia in his self-maternalizing, ends up offering a series of resistances to masculinity, both directly and through ironic self-degradation: he is "beneath manhood" and refers to "my infirmity," his "mental twist," the "symptom of some sickly discourse," all addressed to the male reader ("a busy man, perchance"), to whom he both seems somewhat embarrassed and threatens to "retire, *impenetrable* [my italics] to ridicule, under the phantom cloud of Elia." Time itself is feminized: the old year's "skirts" and the new year's birth.

Perhaps one of the reasons Lamb has been singled out as "dear" and "saintly," what I think are unconscious cognates for queerness, is not simply because readers have given him grief points and responded to his whimsy, but they have subconsciously *allowed* him a resistance to conventional emotional valences they might have found excessive in most male writers, writers working in genres that were, perhaps, less performative. I think this reaches an apotheosis in Lamb in his essay "New Year's Eve."

Whether the essay will become less queer, the more it becomes typed, subcategorized, or postmodernized, or will avail itself of some continuing inner "heresy," to invoke Lukács, is up for grabs. I worry about the essay's domestication, a false sense of formal radicalization. Merely breaking up paragraphs or adding poetry to essays (Cowley did that in the mid-seventeenth century) doesn't make an essay queer or politically resistant once that becomes one of the old bags of essay tricks that all beginning essayists must practice to construct barricades to the paragraph, within whose contours Lamb, Woolf, Baldwin . . . Montaigne, wrote such wild, fascinating, queer words.

Essays on the essay never pin the essay down. A queer theoretical essay wouldn't even want to. But it's worth noting that the essay has always been a site of resistance, a place where things have happened rhetorically as well as formally that haven't happened elsewhere. Sir William Temple, anyone?

READING "NEW YEAR'S EVE"

Reading "New Year's Eve," by Charles Lamb, is a Heraclitian experience—it's so short and emotionally dense, yet its touch is so light that it's difficult for a reader to respond to it in precisely the same way twice. It is a hallmark Elia essay: wry, self-knowing, quirky in its archaic diction, modulated tonally between melancholy and zest. The essay is autobiographical but cautious, as Lamb had right or reason to be, giving no detail that could positively identify the speaker as writer. And yet the familiarity between essayist and reader that Lamb creates is among the most intimate ever created in the form. Lamb's ostensible subject, New Year's Eve and the way it causes us to turn inward, to reflect, is a metaphorical birthday of the year and thus, for us all, is his entry to the actual or deeper subject of the essay, which is his meditation about the ever-nearer prospect of death, his terror of it, and the emotional and psychological conditions around which this fear reverberates. The essay is psychodramatically structured around Lamb's anxiety, but his anxiety extends even further, to his gender and his genre, wrapped as they are around each other in this queer, haunting, and haunted New Year's essay.

The essay begins with its least intimate paragraph, aphoristically, and this paragraph gives us little hint of the quirky Elian character that Charles Lamb usually crafts: whimsical, self-mocking, nostalgic. It's a formal paragraph that sets the time and occasion: the new year that is stirring up our narrator. The first line of the essay has been quoted often: "Every man hath two birthdays; two days, at least, in every year, which set him upon revolving the lapse of time, as it affects his mortal duration" (27). In its last two words, the actual occasion topic of the essay sneaks in, as Lamb tells us that twice a year we are forced to think about time and, therefore, about death. Lamb, as an avid reader of Thomas Browne, may have been stirred by Browne's *Religio Medici*: "Certainly there is no happiness within this circle of flesh, nor is it in the optics of these eyes to behold felicity; the first day of our Jubilee is death." For those readers who aren't versed in Lamb, in the essays of Elia, I need to stop before I delve too far into the meditative essentia of Lamb's world here and talk about what so many critics and friends and fellow essayists of Lamb's have talked about for the last two hundred years.

Or do I? As I begin to write about the mad murder of their mother by Lamb's sister Mary in 1796, when Charles was just twenty-one, and their subsequent life together (Mary was one of the great "mad women" of the nineteenth century, indomitably smart, courageous, tragic) because of Charles's self-sacrificing decision to take charge of Mary to keep her out of Bedlam— Charles himself had suffered severely from melancholy—I feel conflicted about participating in this old biographical chain, fastening on another heavy link of sympathy like a perverse literary burden. It is ironic indeed to create a connection here to Dickens, so influenced by Lamb. I refer, of course, to *A Christmas Carol*, the more widely known of these two nineteenth-century seasonal reflections. Which digression to follow first: Mary or Dickens? Better first to wade into Lamb's new year.

Mary Lamb criticism, as Joseph E. Riehl documents in his exhaustive *That Dangerous Figure: Charles Lamb and the Critics*, is shot through with references to Lamb's past and to his life with his sister. Lamb had taken the knife out of his sister's hand and then had taken responsibility for his sister against his brother John's wishes. For this he becomes canonized by Thackeray as "Saint Charles" and burdened with an anvil of geniality that predisposes his readers to light reading. Elia, his pseudonym, was created to protect Mary, and himself. Much has been speculated about the provenance and etymology of "Elia," whether it was a name carved out of Elijah, a popular name in medieval literature, which would undoubtedly call out to a writer who claimed that he wrote "for antiquity." Lamb was not profoundly religious, beyond what we can know from the work, letters, and biographical information. I was always tempted, because of my own background, to see the ghostly Jewish prophet who is both present and absent at the Passover seder, who comes in and drinks his wine, as Lamb's inspiration. Then last month, looking through one of the many different volumes of Lamb letters I have, I found a letter to J. Taylor, dated July 30, 1821, supposedly explaining Elia (which Lamb tells him should be pronounced *Ellia*):

> Poor Elia, the real (for I am but a counterfeit), is dead. The fact is, a person of that name, an Italian, was a fellow-clerk of mine at the South Sea House, thirty (not forty) years ago, when the characters I described there existed, but had left it like myself many years. . . . I went the other day . . . to laugh over with him at my usurpation of his name and found him, alas! No more than a name, for he died of consumption eleven months ago, and I knew not of it.

Elia was the "author" of *The Essays of Elia*, in which New Year's Eve appeared, in 1823. It didn't take long for Lamb to be out-ed, and considering the care he was trying to take, several friends took credit for the exposure, including Hazlitt. A second volume, *The Last Essays of Elia*, appeared in 1833, the year before Lamb's death, but the jig was long up by then. Elia is a pseudonym, but it would be a mistake to push him too far from Lamb. Reading Lamb's letters, one finds a persona that is a bit sharper, perhaps moodier, more impatient, but clearly recognizable as the central self of the essays.

As for Dickens, *A Christmas Carol*'s nostalgic sentimentality, the message of infinitely possible change, affected me deeply when I was a boy, and I don't wish to whip it because of its sentiment. I used to secretly stay up until all hours of the morning on Christmas Eve watching, on my nine-inch Sony, both the 1935 film version with Reginald Owen and, my favorite, the 1951 version with Alastair Sim. I needed to repeat this talismanically for years in an attempt to re-create my early-childhood delight and wonder, waiting for the presents I received on my brother's birthday, Christmas day—a boon for a little Jewish boy—which my mother would have wrapped up and left mysteriously deep in the night. I imagined her bending over them as though the presents were myself. The repetition of experience, though, gradually faded, when successive lovers found my all-night vigil childish or regressive and I gave it up. As Lamb understood, and I always wonder if Mary did (who can resist trying to enter her mind?), we're sentinels of secret pleasure and regret for our younger selves; but unlike Dickens, Charles Lamb didn't see the past didactically, as the place where one went for answers like the proto-psychoanalytic movement of *A Christmas Carol*'s depth charges that expose Scrooge's anal venality and his paranoia. Rather, Lamb's neurotic retreat into the past is adaptive and pleasurable, consoling, self-protective, even on some level masturbatory since it takes the place of living pleasures. The essential difference between essay and story: Lamb enacts thought and feeling, considers, whereas Dickens narrates symbolic behavior and moralizes. Scrooge and Elia suffer radical ruptures in their pasts involving their mothers' deaths—Scrooge's at his birth, Lamb's at his sister's hand. But Scrooge, the story's antihero turned hero (we utterly respond, on some level, to Scrooge's misanthropy), needs an almost traumatically transformative experience of memory in order to live, whereas Lamb had reason to seek the comforts of the far past in memory in ways he found deeply pleasurable and were necessarily sublimated due to a life deprived of marriage, children, and expressive sexuality—a life of repetitive work and almost constant anxiety. Lamb's presented self-image—celibate, stammering, barbed with wit but openhearted, literate but resistant to literary pretension yet full of archaic and recondite literary taste—challenges categories of class and gender expectations, the role of the writer, the nature of authorship, queering not only himself but the genre as he goes.

The need for pseudonym, the inability to broach certain subjects (why he lived with his sister, why he hadn't ever married, and for that matter why he spent those decades chained to the desk at the East India House, where he tells us so memorably in "The Superannuated Man" that "the wood had entered into my soul"), the changing of names (Mary is his cousin Bridget; his brother John, James Elia), Lamb's subconscious resentment and need to memorialize—all these point to a writer without the liberties we take for granted in our confessional essays today, but whose severe decorum pushed him to write essays subtextually layered, superficially convivial, and elegantly structured, full of gorgeous turns of phrase, but with dark undertones and radical contradictions. Lamb's essay "A Chapter on Ears," for example, belies an abiding horror and fear that he might encounter Mary's . . . well, what do we call it now anyway with retrospective diagnostic sympathy—better to use his own language and just say "madness." "A Dissertation upon Roast Pig," for all its brio (or *gusto*, as Lamb teases Hazlitt in an aside), works partially because Lamb's subtle exploration of the tensions of sublimation that extreme pleasure places on us—sublimations he was intimate with his entire adult life—leaks out into a more severe subtextual fear of madness. As he tells us in "New Year's Eve," even pain becomes pleasure as he relives and rehearses memory with the pleasure that others might savor in new experience. Lamb writes (and let's concede that Elia is his mouthpiece), while acknowledging the persona-lizing; to keep saying Lamb as Elia suggests we know how to pull them, or any essayist's self and persona, apart—the best we can do is look at essays and letters, diaries and e-mails, twitters and blogs to see the various selves an essayist has written): "That I am fond of indulging, beyond a hope of sympathy, in such retrospection, may be the symptom of some sickly idiosyncrasy. Or is it owing to another cause; simply that being without wife or family, I have not learned to project myself enough out of Myself" (28).

There is an embarrassment in the rhetoric of Lamb's essay, the language of illness and excess—and it shows up elsewhere in Lamb—that supersedes the topos of modesty. In "By a Friend of the Late Elia," his auto-da-fé, he writes, "He was too much of the boy man. The *toga virilis* never sat gracefully on his shoulders. The impressions of infancy had burnt into him, and he resented the impertinence of manhood. These were weaknesses; but, such as they were, they are a key to explicate some of his writings." Lamb is being playful but also hiding, as it were, in plain sight. "I am naturally, beforehand, shy of novelties: new books, new faces, new years,—from some mental twist which makes it difficult," he tells us, in the fourth paragraph of "New

Year's Eve," and goes on to say, "In a degree beneath manhood, it is my infirmity to look back upon those early days. Do I advance a paradox, when I say that skipping over the intervention of forty years, a man may have leave to love *himself*, without the imputation of self-love?" (160–61).

Lamb's great maw of nostalgia for the past, that premurderous prelapsarian age ("From what have I not fallen"), becomes an insistence on looking back, looking over his shoulder, not at Sodom, but at Eden. Boy-man that he was, with gender-destabilizing persona (aging celibate bachelor, lover of old china), Lamb is queer or protoqueer. His language of (masculine) degradation: ("beneath manhood," "my infirmity," "mental twist," "symptom of some sickly discourse"), addressed to the male reader ("a busy man, perchance"), to whom he seems somewhat embarrassed and threatens to "retire, *impenetrable* [my italics] to ridicule, under the phantom cloud of Elia," raises the issue of persona; but more importantly it speaks to Lamb's discomfort with his own unstable self (162). Time itself is feminized: the old year's "skirts" and the new year's birth. Perhaps one of the reasons Lamb has been singled out as "dear" and "saintly" as cognates for his emotional intensity is not simply because readers have given him grief points, but also because they have subconsciously *allowed* him the temperament whose valence they might have found excessive in male writers whose queer sensibilities weren't showing.

Of course, the essay itself is a queer genre. It breaks and violates genre norms, destabilizes identity. The essay is not genre normative; Montaigne understood this in 1580. The essay always keeps its narrator in motion, in a perpetual search for the chaotic and fluctuating self. "Our life is nothing but movement," Montaigne writes in "Of Experience." In "Of Repentance," he writes, "I cannot keep my subject still. It goes along befuddled and staggering, with a natural drunkenness. . . . I do not portray being: I portray passing." This sense and re-creation of the self as destabilized creates a genre that resists stability as well: a queer genre, changeable and unstable. And Lamb's gender in this queer essay pulls at the expectations of masculine gender behavior, as many essays do, but more explicitly: a queer essay in a queer genre.

There is great appetite in Lamb, for food and for the past, and insatiable longing. Speaking of Barthes and Proust, other boyish men, Carol Mavor writes of the umbilical ties of mothers to sons: "Scarring, after birth, it leaves its mark, its longing. A 'longing' (as Susan Stewart so eloquently writes) is maternity's 'craving' for its child, and, in turn (I would add) the child's craving for the maternal. Craving becomes a carving. It is a queer 'longing mark.'" Synonymously, she explains, it is an "impression," "the generative metaphor of writing." In Lamb's case, though, he cannot speak of his mother directly, and he virtually never does in his work. Mary killed her, and one imagines that even if it were not for the inhibitions of decorum, he would have shrunk away from the recollection. In fact, he tends to write about other maternal figures instead: his aunt, or Mrs. Whist. In "New Year's Eve" his remembrance of being ill at Christ's Hospital, his school, has him waking to a kind of shadow mother figure—a symbol (or is it himself in memory watching over his younger self?): "I can lay its poor fevered head upon the sick pillow at Christ's, and wake with it in surprise at the gentle posture of maternal tenderness hanging over it, that unknown had watched its sleep" (161).

Or is his longing so deep that he can't say "mother"? What is the word? What is the word, we wonder, like Stephen Dedalus in the Nighttown section of *Ulysses*? Essay? Mary? Some queer vocative? Lamb adopts himself in the essay, adopting, too, a kind of family romance along the way, suggesting the child he "must take leave to cherish"—"that 'other me,'" must be radically separated from the fool of the present. It's a rhetorical sleight of hand, and emotionally extraordinarily complex. Lamb begins this paragraph by speaking of his painful introspection and then tells us both playfully and pointedly how unworthy he is: "light, and vain . . . a stammering buffoon." He unmans himself with self-criticism, a masquerading castration that isn't, however, crippling, but rather transforming. He then turns with tenderness to become the maternal guardian of his younger self. It is as adoptive mother to himself ("and adopt my own early idea, as my heir and favourite") that he cries over his boyhood travails. One of Lamb's "chestnut" lines appears here, measuring his unworthy present to the idealized child: "God help thee, Elia, how art thou changed! Thou art sophisticated" (161). But, in fact, Lamb's identity does not at all seem fixed—maternal, unmasculine, boyish, evasive . . . queer; and desperate to reveal essential elements of himself, Lamb may be sophisticated in the art of the essay, but he knows better than to cast himself as static. The element of Lamb that is most protean, most self-comforting, most able to enter the past, most maternal, most essayistically alive, is also queer. Perhaps we would do him justice to replace Thackeray's "Saint Charles" with "Queer Charles."

Is it any surprise that in *A Room of One's Own*, that primary twentieth-century essay, that androgynous qua queer manifesto, the essayist that Woolf encounters "strolling through those colleges" in the introductory pages of the essay is Lamb? She writes, "As chance would have it, some stray [here she anticipates and links Lamb to the queer Manx, to herself] memory of some old essay about revisiting Oxbridge in the long vacation brought Charles Lamb to mind." "Indeed, [a]mong all the dead," Woolf says, connecting to Lamb as comrade in mortality, a New Year's Evish connection, "(I give you my thoughts as they came to me) Lamb is one of the most congenial: one to whom one would have liked to say, Tell me then how you wrote your essays." The answer she knows, we come to understand, is queerly.

Proust wrote that, "In dying, Maman took with her little Marcel." Our mothers, in birthing us, are bound in complicated ways to the death drive—how much more so in Lamb's case, with much of his life sacrificed to his sister's matricide. In mothering his sister, and his sense of loss, Lamb attends to "the child I remember, if the child I remember was indeed myself" (161). But the child is also parent to his own self-surrogacy, as Lamb questions whether or not this child was not "some dissembling *guardian*" (my emphasis). Lamb both elides his maternal loss and inscribes it. He mutes and holds close the essay's temporal obsession: his abiding but, especially at this darkest time of year, acute fear and loathing of death, which the fractured comforts of memory do not completely allay.

Lamb introduces the subject with a parallel image: "The elders" of his youth celebrated, it seems, much like his friends, with "hilarity" amongst the former and "exhilaration" amongst the latter. But even though Lamb opines on the limits of children, in his case it seems there was a predisposition to introspection, since the midnight bells bring "a train of pensive imagery into my fancy." Lamb dispatches with the clichés of death, which distance and deny experience. The crucial phrase is "he brings it not home to himself," he who, unlike Lamb, avoids language to distill and re-create the pain of what he really feels. For Lamb, death is shudderingly close, "the unpalatable draught of mortality," as opposed to the trivial passing away "like the weaver's shuttle" (162).

What follows, dead center in the essay, is extraordinarily anomalous, considering that Lamb has told us that he has "almost ceased to hope," that he is "sanguine only in the prospects of other (former) years": a short prose poem of joie de vivre, written in very simple language—no Elian archaisms. It is one of my two or three favorite passages in the entire essay canon, I must admit, but it's more than just a personal favorite. It's the great prose ode to satisfaction, to sufficiency, toned by Elian desire to erase time, stop it. Lamb writes:

> I am in love with this green earth; the face of town and country; the unspeakable rural solitudes, and the sweet security of streets. I would set up my tabernacle here. I am content to stand still at the age to which I am arrived; I, and my friends: to be no younger, no richer, no handsomer. I do not want to be weaned by age; or drop, like mellow fruit, as they say, into the grave.—Any alteration on this earth of mine, in diet or in lodging, puzzles and discomposes me. My household gods plant a terrible fixed foot, and are not rooted up without blood. They do not willingly seek Lavinian shores. A new state of being staggers me. (29)

Is Lamb's delicious embracing of life a marshaling of resources? A preemptive ballast? A desire to do away with time altogether, life and death combined? Lamb gives us a list of what he would most miss, fairly generic except for the way "the juices of meats and fishes" run into "society," and his last item: "irony itself." Has any other writer lamented the approach of death because of the death of irony? This is a writer's lament, surely. I would miss irony, too, and charming digressions. One can see in some writers' self-epitaphs and monuments the attempt to squeeze one last ironic moment into eternity: "Cast a cold eye . . ."

Ironically, this comes before Lamb's darkest moment in the essay. Or is it a swing? The incongruous senses of selves, the backward and forward movements, all suggest a self in crisis, rendering an essay that similarly wants to suggest its pain, without giving the fullness or the depth of it, or rather to give voice to despair in glimpses, lines, that are then tonally undercut or grammatically beset. Lamb doesn't seem to want to stray too far from delight, at times, as though darkness and delight were antimonies. But there are moments when "in winter this intolerable disinclination to dying—to give it its mildest name—does especially haunt and beset me" (163). Lamb writes to the dash with negative tension, a line hard to read, whose sense emerges doubly, the multisyllabic middle words acting as resistance to "dying." It is surely not the "disinclination to dying" that is intolerable, but rather the idea of death itself? At least, that is what Lamb tells us in his text. But the sentence is saying that it is the resistance to death, the "disinclination," that is itself intolerable, as though his very resistance has become the problem, tormented. And to be "haunted" is of course to be reminded, and we know about Lamb's ghosts, of the past and of himself. One need only read "Dream Children."

Lamb's funny rebound is delightful and amusing, but over the years, I find it less and less convincing. In a letter to Dorothy Wordsworth, written at Christmas 1822 (Lamb must have sent her a copy of the essay, which had first been published in 1821, or an advanced copy of *The Essays of Elia*, which would be published in January of 1823), Lamb writes:

> I am glad you liked my new year's speculations: everybody likes them, except the author of the *Pleasures of Hope* [Thomas Campbell, Scottish poet and editor of *New Monthly* magazine]. Disappointment attend him! How I like to be liked, and *what I do* to be liked! They flatter me in magazines, newspapers, and all the minor reviews; the Quarterlies hold aloof. But they must come into it in time, or their leaves be waste paper.

"*What I do* to be liked": Lamb's self-aware creation of the beloved Elia/Lamb. He needed a turnaround in "New Year's Eve" to keep Elia reasonably cheerful. So having told us that "antidotes, prescribed against the fear of thee [death], are altogether frigid and insulting," he finds, in the hectoring of "ordinary tombstones," the "odious truism, that 'such as he now is, I must shortly be'"—the animus to push against death: "Not so shortly, friend, perhaps, as thou imaginest. In the mean-time I am alive. I move about. I am worth twenty of thee. Know thy betters! Thy New Years' Days are past. I survive" (163). It's thematically satisfying, but too quick and easy, although I must admit that, at times, I want Lamb to lead me out of the dark spot of the year, out of melancholy, and yield to his emotional quick-change-artist celebration.

Lamb understands that in his substitution of Charles Cotton's poem "The New Year" with his own extended transitional turnaround, he is signaling the depth of his position. Cotton (that early translator of Montaigne) wrote poems that seem terribly unaffected, unmannered, with some lovely plain English prose (I like his use of the word "superexcellently," for example), even if most of the work is not abundantly complex. His "The New Year" replicates the emotional movement of Lamb's essay, more or less, from remorse and regret to promise. But quite frankly, I—and I wonder if this is not the case for many readers—have passed over the poem since the first few times I read the essay. It breaks, and in effect ends, Lamb's essay. At the end, Lamb writes hypercheerfully (superexcellently!) that those "puling fears" have "passed like a cloud." They were "hyponchondries"—at least a faint nod toward the necessary neurosis at the heart of the essay.

But we're urged to drink "a cup of the generous" for the "merry New Year," as Lamb salutes us at the end, "my masters." It's difficult to imagine Hazlitt ever addressing his readers as "his masters." But then Hazlitt may have liked to be liked, but he did not do much to be liked. Which, of course, we also like.

What Lamb did to be liked created the tensions that made essays such as "New Year's Eve" so complex, so strange, so intimate, so capable of working at such different levels. Unlike the chimes that call Scrooge back to a reevaluation of the past, renewed and purged of demons, Lamb gives us a winter picture of the self facing the terror of extinction, the unstable queered self who finds recondite comfort in the past and sees change as deathly. Scrooge seems to beat death, which is why *A Christmas Carol* is sentimental. In "New Year's Eve," Lamb changes the subject. Denial, he knows, is the opiate of the reader, and his readers' approval, it seems, was his opiate.

PLAYING OURSELVES
PSEUDODOCUMENTARY AND PERSONA

In an episode of Larry David's show *Curb Your Enthusiasm*, a Holocaust survivor and a survivor of the TV program *Survivor* go head-to-head about whose struggles were more intense: "I'm saying we spent forty-two days trying to survive. We had very little rations, no snacks," the TV survivor says. "And no gym."

"We didn't eat for a week, for a month," the Auschwitz survivor says, appalled that snacks are the threshold for what is considered survival.

"Did you ever see our show?" the TV survivor asks?

"Did you ever see our show? It was called the Holocaust?" the Auschwitz survivor responds, and it's a chastening, superbly funny response, in the way it compresses moral indignation, the history of the Holocaust's various commercial appropriations, and our own generic double take that we're not even watching a Holocaust survivor, but an actor playing a Holocaust survivor responding to the *actual* TV survivor. Mock doc, indeed, as the *real* Larry David, master choreographer of the awkward moment, playing himself, looks on, horrified.

Curb Your Enthusiasm has many ingredients of the mock documentary, or what I prefer to call the pseudodocumentary;

it is a video-diaristic serial, based on improvisation, recounting the supposed daily life of the show's eponymous creator, Larry David, as he interacts with "real" and fictive personae. The basis of the show is that his main work, the creation of *Seinfeld*, is behind him, and he essentially has nothing to do, wandering around Hollywood aimlessly, occasionally almost starting projects. His Jewishness is well marked, essential, self-branding. At one point, he tells his wife, who has thrown a dinner party conspicuous for its Protestant guest list, "Next time, I want a Schwartz, a Levine," etc.

In *My Dinner with Andre*, released in 1981, Wallace Shawn and Andre Gregory also play themselves—though their Jewishness is unmarked in any direct way, and both men's characters have limitations that are more subtle than Larry David's. Both *Curb Your Enthusiasm* and *My Dinner with Andre* suggest ways in which self-portrayals have evolved, have reached a kind of postmodern apogee. Classically, the self-portrayal (think Montaigne: "it is myself that I portray") was linked to sincerity and authenticity; self-representation, even in the self-portrait, and even when critical or unflattering, or especially so, was read authentically. Cracks appeared throughout the twentieth century: Mark Twain played some version of Mark Twain, a predecessor to Spalding Gray, in hundreds of speaking engagements—not insincere, exactly, but a caricature carved out of himself; George Burns and Gracie Allen were some version of themselves, or not themselves, on radio beginning in 1929 and on TV beginning in 1950 until Gracie Allen's death in 1958; Jack Benny played Jack Benny, a character utterly unlike himself, from 1929 to 1965 on his radio and TV shows; Lucille Ball was Lucy Ricardo in *I Love Lucy*; and lest we forget, Ozzie and Harriet started on radio in 1944 with actors as their kids before Ricky and David took over on TV from 1952 to 1966.

We could add to this endlessly: Robert Benchley playing the drunk Robert Benchley in dozens of one reelers, Orson Welles playing Orson Welles in *F for Fake*, Spalding Gray playing Spalding Gray in successive monologues and movies. The use of "real" names encourages us to read situations as real. The name acts as a kind of truth-bearing halo, covering the actor with the warm glow of truth where it doesn't really belong, in fictive, scripted narratives, while holding tight to the "realness" of its actors, which is to say characters, which is to say personae, which is to say people.

In *My Dinner with Andre*, Wallace Shawn took transcribed tapes of his conversations with Andre Gregory and turned them into a script, which was rehearsed and performed. I call this kind of form pseudodocumentary: it isn't a mock documentary, because its main generic purpose isn't generic parody. It partakes fairly evenly of the conventions of fiction and nonfiction: it is full of autobiographical detail; it also changes autobiographical detail. Shawn and Gregory say they wanted to turn their experience into fiction. But they keep their names. Much the same could be said of Spalding Gray. In the film *Swimming to Cambodia*, he says, "Look, everything I'm going to tell you tonight is true. Except for the fact that the banana sticks to the wall." Well, truth, as we know, is a sticky commodity. And the printed text of *Swimming to Cambodia* is chock full of different versions of events that Gray describes in the movie.

The creation of personae in any nonfiction genre requires the sculpting of a self-aware self-creator. Essaying filmmakers such as Su Friedrich, Ross McElwee, Jonathan Caoette, Alan Berliner, Vanalyne Green, Werner Herzog, create personae of character-narrators who seem unlimited by dramatic irony, who attempt to push past the limits of their problematic relationships, ideas, projects. When dramatic irony does emerge, or the more it does, when "real" characters seem to lack the ability to see themselves as we're seeing them, the closer we come, I would argue, to pseudodocumentary, a form that blends fictive and nonfictive modes and may lean toward contexts or situations that are or seem quotidian: domestic comedies or family shows like those of Benny or Donna Reed, who are forerunners of the surreal and absurd Larry David and Gary Shandling and many of today's reality TV programs.

My Dinner with Andre, for those of you unfamiliar with the film, is essentially a two-character film. The playwright Wallace Shawn and the theatrical director Andre Gregory meet after years of separation, for dinner. Directed by Louis Malle, the film is briefly framed by Shaw's journey to and from dinner, but the preponderance of the film is the conversation during the meal, one of the least mobile films in history, a series of long one shots of Gregory, with occasional shot reverse shots when Wallace interjects and the film becoming more dialogic toward the end. Most of the film recounts Andre Gregory's peregrinations through Poland in search of his missing core self, a very seventies series of post-Esalen encounters, rendered in a kind of shell-shocked mix of wonder and disgust, philosophical curiosity and Western cultural disdain.

My Dinner with Andre was released in 1981, and watching it now, I'm struck by some of the similarities between Andre Gregory and Spalding Gray, in verbal mannerism and visual style. Gray, who was a few years younger than Gregory, came out of a similar experimental theatrical background (and then Esalen), performing with Richard Schechner's Performance Group and later the Wooster Group, which he helped found. Gregory was the founder of the Manhattan Project theater group. Clearly they moved in the same circles. For Gray's theatrical performances, a notebook with a single page of verbal cues would suggest to him where his monologues should go. For the film, these needed to be codified, more scripted, less spontaneous—shots could be set up, so Gray could perform for the camera. He performed himself, in other words, performing a fragmented version of his usual narrating self. And this self, we know, too, was a delightful, interesting construct. Persona always is a construct. Even Montaigne bids goodbye to himself at the beginning of the essays. But how much of an edge, a wedge, is there between construction and character—when does the persona become a character rendered for the purposes of the dramaturgical necessity of the film, and when do we see a more authentic character driving a work for purposes of deeper self-exploration? We know now, for example, that the Spalding Gray we see on film was a constructed persona unfraught by clinical depression. Gray's persona, nevertheless, is complex, full of autobiographical detail. Is *Swimming to Cambodia* Jonathan Demme's pseudodocumentary of Spalding Gray's fractured performance or Spalding Gray's essay film with Jonathan Demme's assistance?

Wallace Shawn, son of William Shawn, had written and produced four plays, including one that had been attacked in the House of Commons for its pornographic content; had been living for some time with the writer Deborah Eisenberg; and was a well-known and ultra-privileged New York literati by the time he appeared in *My Dinner with Andre*. Most audiences remember him from the infamous "homunculus" scene in Woody Allen's *Manhattan* or from *The Princess Bride*. But the film (Shawn himself) presents him as a kind of Everyman, amusingly inarticulate at times.

Shawn turned the transcripts of his conversations with Andre Gregory (who had directed his first play in 1968) into the script for the film, which seems to highlight this idea of the distinction between character and actual or real persona. As Wallace Shawn writes in the introduction to the film script about taking on the project, "I knew immediately that would take forever, and it would really require some brains—I'd have to distort us both slightly—our conflicts would have to be sharpened— we'd have to become—well—characters. . . . It would be an enormously elaborate piece of construction." Ever the imp, Shawn, however, goes on to assert a certain degree of nonfictive validity: "The world of my imagination was becoming a prison. . . . Then suddenly it occurred to me—My God, what if . . . we just did a very simple film . . . in which I would be talking with Andre. . . . And instead of just writing it myself out of my imagination, Andre and I would really talk for awhile, and then my script would be based on our real conversations."

But did the audience know Wallace Shawn to be less Shawn than they knew Jack Benny to be or not to be Jack Benny? Throughout the 1950s a large contingent of the TV-watching audience confused early family shows with self-playing celebrities with pseudodocumentaries. Carl Betz was assumed to be married to Donna Reed. People wondered why Lucille Ball didn't get a bigger apartment. One wonders why Rick Nelson didn't jump out a window before the age of twenty-one.

What does a work's assumptions of our sense of its generic coding matter? *My Dinner with Andre* is a hybrid film. It extracts from old TV shows lurking questions and raises them slightly ahead of its time about the conflation of character and real people. But about real people speaking scripted lines of their own.

In *Broadcast News* (1987), Holly Hunter, raking William Hurt for his acting a reaction shot, says, "I saw the taped outtakes of the interview with the girl. I know you 'acted' your reaction after the interview." William Hurt responds, "I felt funny about it afterwards. It's verboten, huh? I thought since I did it for real the first time . . ." *Broadcast News* takes a conservative position, issues a warning about the dangers of confusing character and the real, about the danger of losing authenticity and objectivity in the journalistic ethos, but the implications are broader. And the floodgates (i.e. reality TV) were about to open.

In *Faking It: Mock-Documentary and the Subversion of Factuality*, Jane Roscoe and Craig Hight write that "like drama-documentary, mock-documentaries are fictional texts, but they position themselves quite differently in relation to the discourse of fact and fiction. In sharp contrast to drama-documentary, they tend to foreground their fictionality (except in the case of deliberate hoaxes)." But does a film such as *My Dinner with Andre* foreground its fictionality or help pave the way for the evolutionary sense of persona as we seem to be experiencing it now, as almost indistinguishable from character in nonfiction? Conventionally, in nonfiction literature, in the essay, we see the persona of the essayist as an extension. We impute truth value to the values we think are true of our narrator. But even here, to invoke Spalding Gray, we're on a slippery slope, going back to Steele and Addison's crafted fictions mixed with real events. The *Spectator* was a pseudodocumentary, sans film and camera. What exactly is "Christ's Hospital Five and Thirty Years Ago," by Charles Lamb. He combines his memories with Coleridge's under the Elian pseudonym. In *F Is for Phony: Fake Documentary and Truth's Undoing*, Alexandra Juasz writes, "Elements that are created for and then marked as serving dramatic purposes locate one place where fake documentary's 'twist' or 'self-conscious distance' rounds off my definition. Like any successful parody, the fake documentary expertly apes the iconic conventions of another textual system, while necessarily marking within the text this doubleness." But I'm interested in those hybrid, pseudo forms that fail to mark their doubleness. How, for example, does *My Dinner with Andre* mark its generic boundaries, mark that Wallace Shawn is the character Wallace Shawn, that Andre Gregory is the character Andre Gregory? How did the reader of Lamb's Elia's Christ Hospital mark his mixed autobiographical and fictive foray? Lamb sent out a dizzying array of possible readings: one reader thinking he was reading Elia, another knowing, as many readers did after a time, that he was reading Lamb posing as Elia, some no doubt, close to Lamb, reading the Coleridgian cues. Others, incapable of doing so, thought they were reading Lamb's autobiographical account.

It starts to seem Oulipolean. Where does genre break, then? If I call *My Dinner with Andre* a pseudodocumentary, is "Christ's Hospital" a pseudoessay? There are other works I could place in that category: David Sedaris, for example, though I'm queasy about insulting Lamb. There are ways in which *My Dinner with Andre* asserts its fictive ontology through the omniscient camera, which moves unseen through the restaurant, that captures the two diners without comment about the means of production, through the fact that we are never acknowledged as viewers but are filtered instead through the limited point of view of Shawn. Adding to this is the film's Holocaust leitmotif and Gregory and Shawn's unremarked background, despite all of the autobiographical detail, as Jews. Like Kaplan, the missing Jew in Hitchcock's *North by Northwest*, Gregory and Shawn are the missing Jews in *My Dinner with Andre*, their own identities marking the real absences of the missing Holocaust Jews Andre seems haunted by. The ontological status of the film becomes strange, peculiar, haunting, when a missing Jew who is playing himself as an un- (as opposed to non-) Jewish character tells us, "I have actually had this very unpleasant feeling that we really should get out [of New York, of all places]. We really feel like Jews in Germany in the late thirties. Get out of here. The problem is where to go." Gregory's traumatic peregrinations, including a symbolic death and burial in a forest in Poland, of all places, aren't cathartic, aren't rejuvenating. Rejewvenating. As Sidra Dekoven Ezrahi writes in the *Yale Journal of Criticism*, citing Geoffrey Hartman, "'We seek,' he says, to 'cut ourselves, like psychotics who assert in this way that they exist. As if only a personal or historical trauma (I bleed, therefore I am) would bond us to life.' As touchstone of our honesty, this 'cut' posits survivor testimony as the most direct encounter that any bystander to history can have with the 'Event,' documentary as the truest form of historiography and strict realism as the discipline for anyone of fictive mind." This suggests the ways that Western culture and media have consciously and unconsciously appropriated the testimony of Holocaust literature, because to have survived has become the pinnacle of existence, the ontological gold medal. Think Gloria Gaynor. Frank Sinatra: "My Way." Larry David: "Did you ever see a show called The Holocaust?"

Gregory interrupts the story of his mock death in Poland:

I mean, who did I think I was? You know? I mean, that's the story of some kind of spoiled princess. I mean, you know, who did I think I was, the Shah of Iran? I mean, you know, I wonder if people such as myself are not really Albert Speer. . . . I've been thinking a lot about him recently. Because I think I am Speer. And I think it's time for me to be caught and tried the way he was. . . . I mean, I would really like to be stripped and unmasked. I feel I deserve it. Because I really feel that everything I've done is horrific. Just horrific.

Gregory's assertion of guilt (he's the wrong kind of survivor) makes him sentimentally as bad as one can be—and since he can't be a Jew, he thinks he's Albert Speer. He's gone the other direction from Cary Grant in *North by Northwest*, who realizes it's better to be George Kaplan than ROT. Than nothing.

But to return to my larger point, my generic point, Gregory and Shawn are dialectical tennis partners who have used themselves, versions of themselves, in a narrative. So what is this narrative?

Vivien Sobchach notes in her essay "Phenomenology of Nonfictional Film Experience," "We must remind ourselves that a 'documentary' is not a thing, but a subjective relationship to a cinematic object." And our relationship to objects changes over time. We know more now about Gregory, Shawn, Spalding Gray, and Charles Lamb than when the works I've discussed were released. Conditions, characters change along with our reception. But the question of the ontological status of nonfiction doesn't seem to want to go away. Persona is never non grata in generic terms.

As for those missing Jews—I see them falling in my dreams like rain, like the geometric (or is it metastatic?) image of bourgeois *gentilshommes* in Magritte's *Golconda*.

Or do I?

THE USEABLE PAST OF M. F. K. FISHER

AN ESSAY ON PROJECTS

I decided not to call; my anxiety regarding immediately awkward encounters coupled with fear (her work was too important to me) added up to the appropriateness of correspondence. This produced a direct and somewhat stiff proposal: can I come and spend weeks interviewing you. M. F. K. Fisher replied post haste from the hospital that "It sounds like an amusing idea in every way." I had proposed a month-long stay. These were the last words in the short note I received back, twenty-five years ago. Teachers and Writers Collaborative had enthusiastically suggested I visit her as a variation on the theme of their Mentor Program: several weeks of interviewing, observing, perhaps helping Fisher where I might. Phillip Lopate had dropped my name with them, mentioned my interest in Fisher, doing me a great favor. I also felt as though I were guiding myself from one mentor to another, the fresh blood of new essays coursing through my veins? As young as I was, I felt too old to be that menu's spring chicken. But I didn't know quite what I was doing, what I was after. I only knew the ostensible reasons for this "project," but hadn't begun actively wondering what I might *really* be doing, or why.

Fisher had interested me for several years. The doyenne of "food writing," she was then the author of fifteen or so books of essays (before the M. F. K. Fisher industry really geared up): memoirs, recipe-essays, food-memoirs, autobiography, travel-essays, travel-food-essays . . . and a brilliant translation of Brillat-Savarin's *Physiologie du gout.* The list is meant to suggest how hard her work can be to classify, to genrify. I had first heard her work when the woman I was seeing, my ex-lover, short-term girlfriend (travel-essay, food-essay, memoir . . .) read "The Flaw" to me. Lest that seem portentous, I hasten to add that it may or may not have been. In any case, the following day or week, on her birthday, she dropped a copy of *The Art of Eating* in my mailbox, inscribed "To David, Who Will Be Forty-Three in the Year 2000." We were in our pursuit of the millennium stage; that's only fun until a relationship hits its apocalypse. I imagine we had been discussing Alain Tanner. She was cooking late dinners for me, hot late Texas barbecues, as we sat on her wooden porch drinking wine. As prose writers, perhaps we were more moon-eared than eyed; we read to each other frequently: Stein, Garcia Lorca, Kafka, M. F. K. Fisher.

A few years later, this personal intimacy having curdled, she wrote a piece about our months together called "The Mockingbird" and had her picture in *People* magazine holding up the story and smiling. It had won an award. I had redeemed myself for her as material. Or so I gather, because she was merely cutting then, as opposed to openly hostile. I say something shockingly unironically in that story. But we hear what others say and recombine their words and tones, their works and days, to square with psychological necessity, and also sometimes to render what works on the page. Sometimes that doesn't square with anyone else's version, old beloveds, current mothers, estranged friends, acquaintances. All this the world knows. Certainly autobiographical writers. But, Christ, it's still shocking to see yourself served up cold.

Fisher had progressed to one of my favorite few, the writers we wrap in sable, or battle out the anxieties of influence or confluence with, perhaps remember when we first read. And then she was "a project," proposed to and agreed with purposively but without a clear object. As such, I thought about it variously as an adventure—a trip back to lovely Northern California, where I had gone to graduate school in the late seventies—and an obligation that I was contracting to fulfill, having been obligingly located on the Great Chain of Writing, rather far down the links. Would I be an amanuensis for a month?

This project, though exciting, sounded potentially difficult, far from an "amusing idea," at least in every way. Reaching Fisher, to begin with, had required some detective work in those pre-Internet days. An acquaintance had given me the telephone number of a friend of her brother's in Paris. The answering machine there referred me to a number in London. I decided against turning the matter over to Interpol. Instead, I stuck with my middle of the night dialing and reached a stranger twice removed who was remarkably uncurious, almost ready to jump off the phone having provided me with the information requested—telephone number and address. The purpose of my request felt like an afterthought. But I forced it on her breathlessly, hoping for preparatory information: an amusing anecdote, a tip on what to say, or whether I should tiptoe or be brazen. She told me to say hello to Mary Francis for her.

~~~

While no one talks about Proust as a food writer because of his memorable madeleine, M. F. K. Fisher gets pigeonholed because she has chosen gastronomy as her central subject, her all-purpose metaphor. Genre nonfiction, as though the progress of an essay were dictated by its subject. But Fisher's gastronomical self always exists contextually within a larger life, food acting as a transport to memory, to a more vibrant experience of life: "If I could still taste my first oyster, if my tongue still felt fresh and excited, it was perhaps too bad. Although things are different now, I hoped then, suddenly and violently, that I would never see one again" ("My First Oyster"). While I may have had clearer ideas than many readers about the vitality of Fisher's work as an essayist, I was also aware that my sense of her as missed and misused was somewhat overstated, a residue of the arrogance of enthusiasm, which can be terribly proprietary. This, too, wasn't uncommon to Fisher devotees. But balancing this detritus was also a core of questions about Fisher's work, which contained subterranean suggestions that I wanted to clarify.

I did not quite think that my mission was quite obscure: I wanted to meet Fisher, whose prose I admired and whose life, carefully revealed, was full of fascinating peregrinations. Having spent what had turned into years writing and reading the essay, I felt attuned to the intimacy between writer and reader that the personal essay so frequently calls for, a relationship poised between identification, intellectual companionship, and surrogacy. The navel of loss: Montaigne tells us that the death of his closest friend La Boétie has left a vacuum, which his essays will partly mollify. Hazlitt is always dropping in asides to tell us what an emotional disaster his life has been, wondering if his disappointment is not universally shared. In Colette's essays, the intimacy between writer and reader is sometimes wicked and sometimes lyrical: isn't it all frivolous and beautiful, she seems to ask us, and we feel our own assent acknowledged by her sardonic winks to the audience. Fashion and fads are ridiculously ephemeral, and so are we. So many essayists create an elegiac undertone as losses are revealed, re-created in the solitude of memory. In my own work, I like dropping breadcrumbs for other neurotic, half-cynical, half-deludedly romantic urban types: little cinematic turns around the corner in memory to see if there's a readerly flaneur out there shadowing me. There is, quite frankly, a comfort in the possibilities of this troubled fraternity.

So, as I thought more about my trip, a question kept circling back to me like a digression that will not have its say and subside. In my (relatively) brief stay with Fisher, could I complete the other end of the circuit between writer and reader, the reader as writer stepping in and finishing the friendship essay, consoling its sometimes real, sometimes fictional call for kinship? Was this, perhaps, her responsive chord, or was my project to a large part becoming projection? Fisher is not an essayist whom I felt intimate with in the way that Flaubert considered Montaigne one of his closest friends. I experienced her more like a relative one wishes one knew better because one is intrigued, but whose power is a bit threatening, an attractively compelling and distant relation. Then again, I had lost my mother a decade before. Would the light distance of a close literary mother finally help salve this wound? (I don't like suspense in essays. It didn't.)

What fascinated me most about Fisher's essays (which she resisted calling essays, preferring the more enigmatic "pieces") was the way she creates a voice that manages to be self-knowing while resisting self-analysis. Fisher's sometimes brutal honesty balances with a revelatory reticence. We are left with fascinating images of a retiring, neurotic, agoraphobic mother, an upstanding, responsible, self-enclosed father, and the Puritan grandmother whose devotion to painfully plain fare would be continually and self-assuredly rebutted by Fisher's nearly sixty-year-long writing life, in which, however, she resists questions that probe her own psychology, questions that question her motivation and reveal the essayist's own darker side, although the world's is abundantly evident.

Fisher's best work is ferociously, viscerally observant: it combines the rhetorical control and force of Orwell with Colette's sense of time, the sensuality of time in the slowed-down moment. Fisher most reveals herself through detail and tone. What she discovers is not explicitly self-revelatory. In other words, Fisher tends to direct us to what she has learned, as opposed to what she has learned about herself. In her essay "Feminine Ending," she is a witness to the strange relationship between her brother and a mysteriously powerful singer, a boy named Juanito, who, it turns out, is a girl in disguise: Juanita. Fisher is grateful as they leave Juanita to resume her chosen role, noting that Juanita/o "would be free again, as much as anyone can be who has once known hunger and gone unfed." The strange girl-boy is universalized in her longing, but we are left with our own not so slight hunger for a sense of the writer's own appetites, especially in this case because the particular beneath the universal is strange and suggestive. An essay about transgendered desire *avant la lettre*, it's part of what makes *The Gastronomical Me* and its sea changes such a mysterious work. What we choose to focus on is always telling. I was eager to probe these ambiguities, scratch the surface of suggestiveness. In other words, to enter the inner sanctum and see what I would be told, and see what I could see.

In a postdoctoral frenzy, two weeks before I was to leave for Glen Ellen, M. F. K. Fisher's Northern California base for her last twenty years, I ruptured my Achilles tendon playing basketball, forgetting that my body had not been cryogenically preserved for the ten years I had spent sitting and reading. Surgery; prognosis: casts for three months. I had been steeling myself as it was for the month-long visit. Although I would not be staying with Fisher, I wondered how inconvenient my immobility would be. Gamely and a little guiltily, I decided to proceed and surprise her with my condition: a statement of nonchalant heartiness. My months-long reveries of trekking to Jack London State Park from my exorbitantly overpriced cabin, and indulging in side trips up and down Highway 1, were out. So it was to be mostly the main event: four weeks of daily contact, now intensified in every way.

The week before I left, I had plenty of time to brood. I kept wondering—bordering on obsession as my confidence shook (I was going lame, not whole, and so less armored than I would have been)—why Fisher so eagerly agreed to have me come. My initial letter had been short and full of vague intentions: "work with," "write about," "also assist where I can." Surely this didn't sound "amusing in every way," a gracious diction, but was it slightly mocking? A controlled openness, perhaps, that ready essay into experience but with extreme self-assurance? Ironic unction? Confident abandon? All exegeses sounded equally intriguing, equally plausible, none more right than another. However, I did *not* plunge into experience readily with extreme self-assurance when I was younger. I tended instead to force myself into new experiences irregularly, and almost ideologically, to put myself in unfamiliar situations, throw myself into the experiential pool. To switch metaphors, this horse was usually pulled by the idea of a cart, but this time the horse was hobbling.

I begin to feel like a biographical *Tristram Shandy*: all lead-up and no birth of the subject. An essay on "projects"? Oh, perhaps. I begin to reexperience my reaction to being in biographical mode: M. F. K. Fisher obliquely suggested I write hers; I was flattered and horrified at the idea of spending years in another life, albeit a fascinating one. Even a small fish swimming near a big fish doesn't want to be inside the big fish. I realize this response isn't inevitably true, but it was the way I felt. I found myself, my response to the world, sufficiently interesting. It also may reflect my sense of life's complications; I have little enough faith in my ability to sort through my own past, but the idea of years-long sorties into another's seems impossible. I have too many ghosts of my own to conjure up someone else's, rattling their chains at every unfair or incomplete characterization.

I finally settled into my lodgings, about a fifteen-minute drive up a curvy mountain road, which I navigated by slinging my encased right leg far left and uncertainly driving with my left. I called for directions—my first call—and spoke to two women: one somewhat abrupt, almost defensive, Californian, and the other inviting, almost teasingly friendly, and recognizably eastern Texan. These would separate themselves, respectively, into Fisher's part-time secretary and nurse-housekeeper-cook. The first sense I had of each was prophetic. The secretary saw me an interloper on sacred ground, a pagan with a dubious sense of the sacred. The nurse-housekeeper-cook, who was outside the loop of Fisher's literary identity and production, treated me with Texan hospitality, in part because I was an outsider too. But the prophecy would also speak to Fisher herself, part warm hostess, part scorpion.

I went to Fisher's house in the late afternoon. It was the house nearest the road, but not too near, perhaps a quarter of a mile. It was quirky, each room multifunctional. A sign on the door urged one to come in without knocking (although this, I'd learn, belied the fact that no one stops by without checking with Fisher's intercessors first). The foyer, painted a burnished red, something close to ochre, was narrow and book lined. A door opened to Fisher's bathroom/art gallery, equally dark, where almost all wall space was covered with paintings—from folk to modern art—and memorabilia. The long tub had curtains on either side, roped back. The counters—stretching twenty, twenty-five feet?—were lined with makeup and medicine. The effect was movie elegant, the bath of Carole Lombard, but quirkier. Jean Arthur? Sexier. Garbo. But Fisher didn't quite want to be alone.

To one's right, from the foyer, down two stairs, was the kitchen/dining room/living room. It was an enormous room, high ceilinged and airy, thanks to the light from the adjacent veranda, filtered in from the foothills. The fireplace was set back, as if to make no undue claim on the kitchen part of the room. On the far left as one entered was one long side of appliances, sink, counter space, whose eye-level windows revealed a shaded bower, a less-commanding, more intimate view than the dense and hazy hills. The veranda was overcrowded with wicker chairs and settees, framed by two high daybeds. The afternoons are hot there, near Santa Rosa, in the summer, and the house lights were kept off to keep the heat back, to attempt an illusion of coolness, which in concert with the amber tile floors almost worked. This veranda would be my spot for dead times, when Fisher was working or resting or when my swollen foot demanded an elevated respite. The kitchen was kept by Nina, the aforementioned Texan, hospitably, informally. It was a place to wander into for teasing chats and refilled glasses of wine, respites from the intensity of Fisher's room.

I was never quite sure if Fisher adored Nina or tolerated her; expressions of both seemed equally vehement.

Turning left at the entrance to the foyer led one to Fisher's bedroom-study, the nerve center of the house. It, too, was dark (in addition to the heat, Fisher's eyes were sensitive to light: a product of Parkinson's disease). The lower ceilings here showed off the rich redwood beams that Fisher selected when she designed the house in 1971, eighteen years before I arrived, leaving the execution and construction to her friend David Bouverie, on whose sprawling ranch the house sits. There were bookcases everywhere, organized in idiosyncratic sections: poetry, eighteenth-century prose, books on Gypsies.

At the far wall was Fisher's hospital bed, with small windows at the foot and head. Light was censored, but Fisher had a keen ear, which kept current with the calls of mockingbirds and the strange buzzing we decided were wasps, perhaps in the wall.

At the center of the room, its back to sliding glass doors and a view of the front of the house, was the hydraulic chair where M. F. K. Fisher spent most of her days. She would frequently ask me to sit here or in her wheelchair, almost coddling my temporary incapacity, at other times forgetting it. "Write about it, about not being able to walk," she would tell me, "a paragraph every day. How you hate it, and how it frustrates you, and how you love it. It would be the nucleus of a book." She'd point to a corner where her albums and tapes were (Jelly Roll Morton, Mozart, Fats Waller, Bach . . .), "I'd like to arrange this corner of the room, but I can't."

When I first walked into her dim study, I saw immense eyes and two arms lifted in greeting. I staggered forward on crutches and took her hands. Implored to sit and tell the sad story of my injury by her whisper of a voice, I did so. I was a little shocked by how frail she at first seemed: thin arms and legs, her vitally expressive mouth and opaque eyes, wheelchair and walker nearby. There's something about a beautiful old woman that has always turned me inside out, and Fisher was transcendently beautiful, wrecked. As it turned out, neither of us had quite prepared the other for our physical conditions: mutual determination, perhaps, or denial?

After some pleasant chatting, Fisher matter-of-factly demanded that I make myself at home for the duration and continued dictating to her part-time amanuensis: a short piece requested by the *Times* that centered on her father, Rex, and her family's casually complicated religious affiliations. This went on for an hour or so, after which Fisher asked me to read the "piece" back to her. She then directed me to cut it. Over time, as one might imagine, I have grown unused to performing on demand, on the spot. I first began to think seriously of writing when it seemed I would more or less always be able to retreat into solitude to work under self-generated pressure. This is a charming idea to someone who is a tad on the anxious side. At my worst, I'm capable of picking up the phone with, "What's wrong?" Fisher's request, a test, threw me into a regressive panic. I didn't experience an anxiety of influence. More like the cognition of pure dissonance: being faced with paring down Fisher's exactly written prose (composed as she dictated, like late James) was terrifying, not simply because she was M. F. K. Fisher but because her prose was dauntingly different from my own excessively elaborating style, which depends on strings of dependent clauses, constant qualification, elaborate digression, and, well, you get the picture.

The essay was ostensibly about her early experiences with wine and focused on her father's procurement of communion wine and the heady mixture of irreverence and church society that surrounded Fisher as a child. I felt the focus on her father was diluted, so I cut a few lines here and there. I sipped the dry

Chablis that was given when I arrived. (When I am offered something to drink in an unfamiliar setting, be it morning or midnight, I always accept, wanting to appear game.) The Chablis went to my head, did nothing to staunch the conspiracy of heat and nervousness. The Chablis may have been dry, but I was starting to drip. Finally, almost drenched, I read back the new version to Fisher. Cut another page.

My concentration must have dried my clothes; perhaps I heated up and dried them out. She seemed . . . not quite pleased, rather mutedly satisfied, perhaps the mark of someone grown used to delegation. Still, I had passed.

The role of guest, especially in unfamiliar territory, on unstructured terms with unfamiliar people, has always been difficult for me. Although I was not staying with Fisher, I started spending six to eight hours a day at her house. In the role of guest, I have always had to fight my natural inclination to be so perfectly unobtrusive, so sensitive to the needs of my host, that it is hard to relax. I always try to be the perfect guest, the guest of whom my host would say, "That was the perfect guest." Of course, I think that the perfect guest needs to not be stiff at all, so that makes it incumbent on me to show that I'm reasonably relaxed. Can you see, can you see how exhausting this is? Consequently, in new situations, intimacy doesn't always burst out of the gate when I'm staying with people I don't know well, but rather in small outbursts of subversive sarcasm, comments loaded with subtle interlinear suggestions that I hope will lead to parrying, a parade of anecdotes from my standard anthology. Superficially, Fisher and I appeared ill matched. Her personality, from the first and thereafter, seemed to be a fascinatingly polarized combination of elegant, nurturing, slightly distanced motherly concern, and waspish wit, indomitable, at times imperious, proclamatory. However, balancing her authoritative power was a tendency to contradict herself. It was as though Fisher tried out a position, as forcefully as possible, and let it briefly gestate to see how it sat. Or did she, I wonder, simply forget, displace, or misplace her original sentiments and engage opinion and feeling as they occur. Was she just a bit capricious? M. F. K. Fisher had her share of fixed opinions and imperfect sympathies, but she seemed suspicious of certainties, which I liked. Commenting on some very early writing experiences, she told me, "I realized I didn't know anyone but myself, and I hardly knew that." Having fought her way through the intricacies of other cultures, the necessities of decades of freelance writing as a means of performing her craft and supporting her daughters and herself, and the nearly debilitating double deaths, months apart, of her brother David and second husband Dillwyn Parish, Fisher acquired, I felt, a certain stoic skepticism within the heart of her love of the sensuous world, what George Orwell called "solid objects and scraps of useless information." Supple ideas are a large part of this world, to be savored in company and to one's own Lucullan delight, and to coexist with contrasting, even antithetical flavors. Since Fisher had no system of ideas (perfect for the essayist!), intellectually or gastronomically, other than accepting and understanding one's multitudinous appetites, perceptions and positions could be momentary experiences, subject to changing circumstance and mood. Perhaps what she communicated as contradiction, therefore, was merely the forceful expression of the instability of experience, both savory and unsavory.

But some of this is speculative. I feel, and frequently felt, that I am losing Fisher as I try to probe more deeply into her consciousness. She would encourage and divert complex reactions, creating weblike caesuras in the blink of a conversational eye. At one point, talking about some painful moments from childhood and what she had written about them, she said, "I thought that would prove things did happen to kids, and they remember. I knew that I knew. It was painful, though, to sort out what I remembered. In desperation sometimes I called on my subconscious when my memories were not being told things. I had a vision of sitting on some rocky pebbles. The game I was playing was saving their lives. But subconscious investigations can be so speculative and turgid. I really haven't fussed with them too much." Fisher spun out tantalizing revelations and undermined them with dizzying frequency, my sense of her flowing and ebbing with a sometimes maddening fluidity.

Still, I try to push through defenses and the welter of stories to focus my impressions, to make connections between the woman I encountered and the work I believed I am familiar with. M. F. K. Fisher was not a sensualist, despite the rhetoric of her reputation. The struggle one senses in Fisher's work and self-presentation revolves around a matrix of complex relationships, some inherited, others chosen. Sensuous pleasures can be self-justifying, but they also underscore shared experience and wrap memories around solitary ones. I struggled, through the mornings and afternoons, to understand the tension in what I was doing between the shared and the solitary, between my interactions, conversations, and my solitary observing self, the self supposedly searching here, sent here for . . . something. I pushed against my own defenses to connect who I am, the work I am doing, to connect the roles of guest, interviewer, potential friend, acolyte, sometime helper, literary critic, essayist.

~~~

Pleasures of the palate are complicated, problematic, revealing. Gastronomy, of course, is M. F. K. Fisher's all-purpose metaphor. As she told me, "I could have written about anything."

Appetite, developing and empowering one's ability to discriminate among the varieties of sensation served forth, is surrounded by the actual complications of mortality, gender, history, and culture. In *On Love*, Stendahl tells us that the diminution of love frequently occurs when repeated experiences fail to evoke the original feelings accompanying the original experiences. We experience a fall, out of love and innocence.

In "The Flaw," an essay in *The Gastronomical Me*, Fisher recounts a repeated trip on a train to Italy in 1939 with her terminally ill second husband, Dillwyn Parish (called Chexbres throughout Fisher's work: "I think I got that from *chevre*, French for goat, because he looked like one"), her greatest love. In the middle of personal tragedy, they are well aware of the looming conflicts on the world stage. Old pleasures, a bottle of Asti Spumante, recognition and attention from the old acquaintance-ship of waiters are tasted, reaffirmed, but somehow intangible as the "doomed" (her word) couple go in and out of tunnels, in and out of childlike delight and aged awareness, "as if we were imbeciles of royal blood, or perhaps children who only thought they had gray hairs and knew how to survive train trips alone." The essay reaches its climax/nadir when they are privy to, and almost witness, the apparent death of a young political prisoner who had attempted a suicidal escape. What they see are the garish remains of glass and blood, artifacts of fate, struggle, and defeat.

What is "the flaw"? A guiltless original sin that demands that one partake of loss on every level? Or is it the very idea of refuge? I inquired, with a sense of mission, since it had been (continues to be) a favorite essay, and central, I thought, to *The Gastronomical Me*. Fisher, as usual, would not remember the specific piece. I began to see her as a kind of literary Lot, not wanting to look back at her work, perhaps aware of the way memory tends to freeze into salt sculptures when written and reconsumed. She would gladly and fully remember events, but would not remember (refuse to remember?) what she had written; she refused or denied the memory of memory, that important and revealing and secondary function of analyzing what we have remembered. It seemed as though this process was an obscuring complication, an obstruction to reclaiming memories purged of earlier versions. An actress who doesn't see her films . . . or a writer who doesn't ever look back at her work?

In reading over M. F. K. Fisher's work, and spending days and weeks with her, I was constantly stonewalled on questions of form. Fisher's attitude, delivered coyly or dogmatically, or turned back to the interviewer, was "I have written a memoir and much journalism; call it what you will, dear, what you feel you must—it matters not to me." I began to feel like a vessel of stories, like a biographer without portfolio. What was I doing there, exactly? Our conversations were surreal at times. I found myself sitting in a wheelchair in a dark room, sweat teasing down inside my cast, listening to someone talking to herself, words, sentences swallowed by the Parkinsonian whisper that would come on frequently in the afternoons. Then a remark, a riposte would be presented to me for acknowledgement, with the direct gaze that implies, "I know you know what I mean, and that is why you are here, because I needed someone who can catch the bird in midflight." And I responded to that need, the pathos of that need to be seen, and to her brilliance. I had been imported, my request a Lacanian inversion.

A conflict of concern to me, how much and in what ways do we self-scavenge, use our lives? The question of decorum. Autobiographical writers can run the risk of Rasputin, whose "The greater my sins, the greater my repentance" mocks the model of Augustinian confession by suggesting, cynically, the utility of his sins. M. F. K. Fisher's essays, poised and elegant, a bit of Hemingway, more than a bit of Colette, are the antithesis of confessions—they forward move almost musically, as curiosity emerges through her outward eye, which wanders until it marks a target, a symbolic image or description of behavior: "I could see only the two people across from me (I knew already that he was a dentist from Monrovia), and maybe one-third each of three people in front of me, but I watched the little dapper steward flicking his tail up and down the aisle, carrying trays and trays" ("The Measure of My Powers, 1941," *The Gastronomical Me*). Moments are rarely interrupted with longer fugues of reflection. The focus is much more often on Fisher's movement through the world than her place in it. It began to make perfect sense to me that she was a parvenu of mysteries, that shelves full of Simenon greeted one in her beautifully muted foyer as if to announce to the unwary that mysteries were revealed only to the astute detective. To a deflective end, both in her work and conversationally, Fisher would sift through potent and tantalizing memory with generous detail while resisting self-analysis. She could talk about herself, write about her life, without a hint of self-indulgence, because her specific motives were not problematically necessary to what she wanted to say, in conversation or prose. She had the least neurotic presentation of self and one of the least idiosyncratic styles of any essayist I can think of. This, in fact, may be why she so resisted my classification of her as a personal essayist, preferring to call her individual work "pieces." Her personal essays work against the traditional strategy of the form: against personality as expressed by idiosyncratic self-interrogation. This conflict, it emerged, is the reason for her antipathy to Charles Lamb. "He's too whimsical for me," Fisher said one afternoon while we were wondering what I might read to her. She said she preferred his letters, "more cool and serious when he wasn't putting on a show."

I began to wonder if my own cool and serious demeanor was part of the interest I seemed to hold for her in those moments when Mary Frances (the personal form that prevailed, a misleadingly genial moniker) suggested that we shared likenesses, that she felt I understood her. But I also was experiencing myself as a rather dull guest, asking the predictable follow-up questions, posing, qualifying, suggesting. This took its toll. My ego was informing me that this project was ill conceived, that I was too self-concerned to be a supporting character for a month. The sidekick role hasn't been my forte. You know, I can pull it off for a little while . . . I would struggle back to my cottage on stilts, pop a codeine pill, sip the requisite Chablis, watch the day moon darken over the Glen Ellen vineyards. I was extravagantly happy to not have to attend to someone else. I was exorbitantly happy with the codeine. I was alone on a beautiful mountain. I had all evening to read, would tell myself that I had the next day planned with a fiercely witty woman who used to play chess with Man Ray.

I felt amorphous. I wanted to go home.

We spent time on the motives of others, as I pressed Mary Frances about the emotional world she had inhabited: sisters, mother, daughters, father, husbands, brother, others. The psychological profile manqué that would emerge would sometimes be summarized abruptly, or dismissed summarily. "She was really just a Victorian afterthought," Fisher said of her mother. Of a friend: "It's simple, really. No inner resources" (John Berryman, anyone?). She ended one conversation with a bombshell: "There was always a strong attraction between Nora [her sister] and David [brother]. I wonder if they ever slept together. Don't think so."

Was she trying to shock me? Was I the object of study? As though she were reading my mind, one evening as I was preparing to leave, to wind my way up the mountain and hop up my set of stairs, she seemed to sense my distraction and difficulty, and astonished me; she took my hand warmly, looked at me with the kind of complete directness that signals attachment, and said, breathlessly, "I've always been detached; that's why my memory is so clear. A little like a ghost." And I felt overwhelmed by the force of her revelation and the strength it had taken for her to reveal, unveil. I nodded awkwardly as she released my hand and almost smiled, slyly, intimately, conspiratorially. Am I being thrown a bone of revelation? Is this a dear gesture? My own detached self was moved. My moved self was suspicious of its suspicions. The tensions between inner and outer worlds take many forms.

~~~

M. F. K. Fisher used detachment, I think, on her many peregrinations. Like many familiar essayists, she resists the world and wanders out into it, curious, suspicious. At the end of "Sea Change, 1937–39" (*The Gastronomical Me*), she says of sailing back to New York with Dillwyn Parish, "Even when New York loomed near us, we felt outward bound. I bit gently at my numb fingers. I seemed beautiful, witty, truly loved . . . the most fortunate of all women, past sea change and with her hungers fed." Fisher's personal quirkiness, I came to realize, was expressed by those contradictions—apparent contradictions at least—of feelings or ideas that she seemed to experience naturally. She was sometimes full of almost-rigid decorum, perfectly comme il faut; at other times, free spirited and nonchalant. Our times together were unpredictably strained or relaxed. I exasperated Fisher with my ineptitude in following her directions for typing out a note of correspondence; later we sat in the dark talking like old friends, with refrains marking the movements of the moon, everything said in a quietly preludial tone. We started switching seats to share the best view and laughed to ourselves about it, as though it were a game, a disabled old woman and a hobbled young man. Her reactions to an old acquaintance were a withering summation: he was snide, pompous, disagreeable. She later described his personality as venal, then urged him to return. She urged me to keep asking questions while she ate and suggested, a moment later, that I talk instead, that I was acting rather graceless, impolite.

Once a group of five women from Nashville fluttered in, laden with food and laurels. They paid homage hyperbolically, as to a demigoddess—somewhat understandable since those on a pilgrimage will act as pilgrims. Sitting on the veranda, as dusk and silence came on and compliments seemed to exhaust, one said to Fisher that if she were to come to Nashville, she would be treated as a queen. Said Fisher, in stage sotto voce, "That's another good reason for not going to Nashville." Later she said, strangely with both generous humor and a dollop of sarcasm, that these fans are nuisances and that oh, they mean well, but they understand very little about anything. And, by virtue of what, I wonder, am I among the cognoscenti, part of the inner sanctum's inner circle?

Perhaps because that muddled middle ground—where most essayists battle toward a complex self-image—is mostly invisible, understandably some readers engage in paroxysms of projection. Fisher, in her work *and* in private, seemed sure of who she was; it was and is the world that offers confusion. Because of her friendship with Janet Flanner (Genêt in most of her Letters from Paris, which appeared in the *New Yorker* for decades) and her psychologically astute portraits of women (Fisher was currently working on a volume of memoirs focusing on landladies), I met avid fans who insisted she was lesbian—her work is certainly full of queer suggestion—and she appeared on her way to iconic status there, too. Writers (not books), it seems to me, are mostly either fetishized or ignored. Perfect subjects for projection: was there one at the heart of my project?

As I look back on my journal of a month in Glen Ellen, hobbling between my second-story apartment in the hills and Fisher's cool valley ranch house, I see not only the struggle to get a sense of who she was and how I might act in her presence but how my own mind worked in relation to her. For example:

7/27/89
Here I am, sitting while Fisher types. She's trying to write a piece about a courtyard in Dijon. Had me read what she had typed out. Difficult to reconstruct in places. Full of precise description, but a bit arid, characterless at this stage. She asked what I thought. I suggested she walk it through to keep the perspective from jumping so much. I'm not sure what she wants to do, but she's hunting and pecking away. I'm facing her. She sits perpendicular to me. I'm in her wheelchair, she in the wicker, her mouth slightly open, occasionally mouthing. She stops, runs her hand over the keyboard lightly to start again as if the moving hand itself did the writing. Her gray hair is soft and thin and tousled. A white cardigan, her long cotton dress with blue and pink and green stripes, narrow and wide, over off-white. Pink slippers, white stockings. She's doing poorly speaking today. I can barely understand her. But this morning she is writing.

Anxious to pick up the thread again at the tantalizing point where we left it—the counterpoint in her family. Gwen [her "aunt," a family friend], Rex [father], Edith [mother], Grandmother Holbrook. I suggested a strange balance: Gwen and Holbrook, Rex and Edith. "It's much more complex than that," she suggested. I want her to go on, to talk about what she sees as her own work's crucible. As does everyone else, I have my own ideas. (And what would I say the crucible of my own is? I have said, of course. Do we demystify our own work uselessly when we try to peg it and create self-conscious themes, make the perfectly implicit, the obsessively understated, too obvious?) She's self-conscious about her work when she wants to be, said to me that she can assume the role of innocence or experience. Today she mentioned that she had never lost her innocence as a reader, while also averring that "I don't read novels anymore. It's hard to get interested in the characters. I focus on the structure." Hardly a sign of innocence. Ruthlessly honest, or . . . determinedly elusive?

We found time in the afternoon, though. She startled me brilliantly: "Nobody ever knows the limits of what another person can stand," she said. "Most suicides are cruel, selfish. Death left me crippled. Timmy's death [Dillwyn Parish] preceded David's death by several months. Part of me didn't survive it."

I asked her about the part that did survive, what that part was. "Anything worth writing about is full of ambiguity," she said. Then she asked me again, in a tone close to an oft-repeated joke, what exactly I was doing here, what I would write. "An essay about spending a month with you," I said. "We'll know each other better after you've written. I feel like I know you very well and not at all," she responded. And that was true. And of course in that moment, we did know each other in a limited essential way at the same time as we both were probing our own ground in a much less limited way. I felt that I was sounding depth charges without giving much away, but that her own sense of detachment appreciated that tact, a kind of reverse-telescopic view, which confirms the object but does not bring it closer in. One could call that tact.

Fisher later explained that she had never written about her tragedies because of a sense of literary decorum. Far from believing in taboo subjects, she had never found a sufficient reason for explicitly using them, although they appear as shadows—dark tones and oblique allusions. I gathered that she hated the thought of such bleak narratives being dredged up for intrinsically therapeutic reasons. In her canon of words, both spoken and written, "dignity" appears with compelling frequency. It is the usable past that concerns her. She spent hours and hours filling me in on the stories of her family, baroque, richly told stories, punctuated by her highly epigrammatic conversational style. Of her first husband, Al Fisher, she said, "He thought he was the only person in the world who had talked to a whore without sleeping with her."

M. F. K. Fisher told me she hoped to live five more years. She lived three. Highly sensitive to the ways those around her faced death, she said she considers her own as a "last great adventure." "I look forward to it," she said one afternoon, as the light in her bedroom/study grew equivocal: "I want to be conscious of the experience. I have no idea what to expect. I only wish I could write about it."

~~~

There were many amusing moments in my month with M. F. K. Fisher: giddiness over strange old recipes for gruesome-sounding dishes, reading essays from the *Spectator* . . . But I suspect I frustrated her by remaining somewhat enigmatic, the good guest with an unclear agenda. His project unperformed? I could blame it on youth now that twenty years has gone by, but my relationship to my younger self is too complicated. I suspect our occasional acknowledgements of affinity were willed, leaps of faith. I also think they were, they felt, entirely real, even as they sometimes felt once removed.

"I'm still not exactly sure why you came," Fisher jibed in a letter several months after I left, wondering between the lines where the work on her was. But in close contact, nothing can stay completely obscured. I believe we came to know each other more than we each supposed, by following clues, ubiquitous and sometimes unreliable clues, to the inner sanctum of motivations. Isaac Babel informs us of the necessity of doing the impossible, "You must know everything." I was reminded of that, one late afternoon with Fisher, when I asked if when she had been able to read, before the ocular encumbrances of her disease, she had spent much time with Montaigne. She replied, "I've never read very systematically. I just read what I wanted to read." A slight smile crossed the corners of her lips, as she paused. Then, "I've read everything." We were both amused; we were both intrigued by her. I shifted my damaged leg awkwardly as M. F. K. Fisher continued to smile inscrutably.

ON MENTORS

A mentor relationship in its conventional incarnation suggests primacy, a spawning born of a teacher's experience and the student/disciple/novice's enthusiasm. To switch metaphors midstream, there is a messianic aspect to the mentor relationship— the student chosen for his or her potential to ascend, the mentor for the aura of infallibility bestowed by position, forgetting the fact that he or she had also, at some point, risen. A secondary influence, anything less than central falls short of mentoring. The influence sometimes has a more holistic, a more transcendent effect; there are mentors whose influence goes far beyond specific disciplines. One might call this mentorship with legs. These are the mentors that Chesterfield wishes for his son, and they are closest to the original sincerity of the moral and spiritual influence Mentor exerted on the supposed Telemachus.

The classic mentor narrative is hierarchical. This, as should be obvious, has been a masculine narrative: surrogate fatherhood intensified by the aura of art. Recently, however, other models, other stories have emerged, in part because of the emergence of women's stories of mentorship, sometimes less fraught with the psychological complexities, the Oedipal complexities of male mentor narratives, sometimes not. Another difference,

I would argue, is the decentralization of the literary world. T. S. Eliot's reign as the Great White Mentor of twentieth-century English literature has long faded. Eliot himself spun a convoluted mentorship web, supplementing G. E. Moore with Pound, whose relationships with Yeats, Ford Maddox Ford, Wyndam Lewis, and Mussolini make him the champion of complexly mutual mentoring in the twentieth century. An honorable mention goes to the convoluted reciprocities of Bloomsbury. Of course, every movement has influences testing, even violating, generational and other boundaries, its literary cross mentoring. The Romantics, Pre-Raphaelites, the odd currents of the fin de siècle in art and literature . . .

The history of the apprentice system, from specialized manual skills to formalized guilds, the initiations of religious acolytes, workshops of artists . . . are only some of the more obvious examples of institutional mentoring. Nevertheless, mentoring through institutions is complicated, intensified by the competition and expectations that swirl around structural power, no matter how petty the forms they take. In lean times, or when there are too many egos to feed, or the double threat of both, there can be a hungry grappling for even small kudos, and the demand for special attention can turn into a feeding frenzy. The nurturing we associate with the mentor/acolyte relationship can turn into something desperate, needy (on either end). Think *The Sweet Smell of Success*. Writing mentors are frequently in a position to feed the fish, and the frenzy. As such, students who enter the academic writing community through writing programs may expect to find a ready-made mentor waiting at the end of the stream. But there is a limit to how much mentoring even the most Mr. or Ms. Chipsian personality can provide. The dirty little secret is that the two factors that most determine the cementing of the mentoring relationship for the mentor are the promise of the mentee and . . . the other is, well, personal, chemical, like love.

The desire for a mentor, the latent desire for surrogate parenting mixed in with a dash of eros (almost everything is), can create a deep yearning for that one person who will provide some answers, some direction, some reward. Have you ever heard a friend say, forlornly, "I never really had a mentor"? Looking for Mr. Goodmentor, as opposed to discovering a mentor, can be frustrating because of that chemical, slightly mystical element in the mentor relationship that resists expectations, immediate mentorfication, and because of the serendipity required for the meeting. "Single white man ISO mentor, 40–60, tall, nonsmoking, into James Baldwin, Jeanette Winterson, magical realism, constructive criticism, monogamy." It's witchcraft, in a sense, perhaps even more so in those mentor relationships that stay somewhat formal, slightly distant; the shine of the coin doesn't dull through overfamiliarity.

~~~

Mentorship, even in its most traditional invocation, requires some degree of personal involvement. There is a sliding scale of how personal mentor relationships become. They can then take on the relational complexities of any combination of teachers, students, friends, parents, children, lovers, all wrapped up in one package, with the extra psychological weight of the mentee's investment in his or her work. Of course, set off against these possible psychic gymnastics are those relationships that are well-defined, straightforward (good fences make good mentors?), which we remember with simple, strong affection and respect. But my own sense of skepticism suggests that the more important a relationship, the more it will tend toward tangling, intricacy, complexity. If it's important, it's fraught. Call this the Second Law of Mentorship. I don't quite remember the first law.

If one believes in an erotics of teaching, in some form, then I think mentorship in its most powerful form is singular, monogamous if you will. It's requited. One can have many teachers, multiple and various influences, but to speak of more than one mentor seems excessive, even a bit intellectually or emotionally promiscuous or unnatural, like having been birthed by two mothers. An exception, I suppose, would be in distinct periods of one's life, if one were lucky enough to have grabbed the psychic and intellectual gold ring more than once. Certainly, it would make sense that some people are more attractive to mentors as acolytes than others.

Can one have been a mentor unawares, and can mentorship be ascribed where it is unacknowledged, even resisted? The first question is easy, even comes with a cliché: "You don't know what your work/class/inspiration meant to me." This kind of mentorship, like gratitude, is in the eyes of the beholden. Some mentors are dead mentors, reanimated in the life of their work. Dorothy Parker claimed to reread Thackery constantly, before and after she wrote for *Vanity Fair*. Montaigne, saddled with the paternalistic moniker "Father of the Essay"—a supposedly first cause creator—was mentor and friend to Hazlitt, Flaubert, and countless other writers. And, of course, Harold Bloom has anxiously explored the implications of some of these questions (Alice Walker less so). *Anxiety of Influence* seemed so, um, seminal, when it first appeared. Much has been written critiquing the masculinist conceptualization of Bloom's work, by Carolyn Heilbrun and others, though I do think Bloom highly alert to the psychological pyrotechnics of possessing an intellectual mentor. I might only add that in the *Oxford English Dictionary*, the entry under "mentor" is "mentulate." Misprision?

Here I should add the exception that literary mentors might be plural. I think we may have that one writer who is our muse (can you pick one?) or we may not.

The search for mentors past can be literally or figuratively proprietary. In the former case, one can lay claims to mentorship through, for example, the purchase of publishing catalogues, including copyright, as Michael Jackson did with the Beatles. A privilege of ownership: the acquisition of art's aura through association. If the purchases are large enough, and the artist still living, the admirer becomes the patron, a role rife with mentor potential, at least in terms of enablement, that has more often yielded to commodification, straight sales: Getty, Annenberg, Rockefeller. This can take less materialistically stellar forms, of course: an autograph, a print, a first edition. You can buy and sell your mentors—psychologically enabling, or another jump down the reification hole? Many years ago, when I was much enamored with his charming poetry, I purchased several of Kenneth Patchen's works on paper. Alas, I read Patchen very little these days, but I still love the Klee and Blake influences and strong colors and surreal aphorisms of the pictures. Mentorship can have false starts that, in the long term, yield to congenially off-centered affinities. But I was a bit of a slut with my literary mentors, worshipping and then discarding idols until my tastes refined. Though, as with Hazlitt, some of my earliest loves remain: Sterne, Eliot, Woolf, Yeats . . . In my twenties: Montaigne, Hazlitt, Lamb, M. F. K. Fisher.

Sometimes we experience the proprietary toward our literary mentors with a hoary cliché: "The work speaks to me," as though sub rosa. It can be telling, obnoxious, but also satisfying to learn that no one understands the distant mentor as truly or deeply (occasionally as madly) as the admirer. In the case of John Clare (which is to say in my case)—who attempted to complete Byron's *Childe Harold*—one may even think, through a deranged process of transubstantiation, that one has become one's own mentor. For about a year, in my early twenties, I was writing John Clare poems.

~~~

Mentorship, as in *influence*, as a writing topic is more rare than one would think. Partially, no doubt, because it intrudes on the Promethean myth of creativity. What creator needs a boost over the wire fence of ignorance, of political, logistical, or neurotic obstacles? To discuss the mentor relationship center stage may invoke feelings—to invoke another myth—that one's rugged individualism is neither so rugged, nor so individual. So you didn't climb the fence by yourself! You were handed a pair of wire cutters, given a leg up! Which may translate, in those dark soliloquies, as, I slipped through? The one-upmanship of hard-knock stories and the fragility of egos are nowhere stronger than among writers, engaged as we are in the least collaborative of enterprises. The difficulty of being here is psychically supported by the difficulty of getting here.

The amount of help admitted publicly by writers is usually finely calibrated. This seems especially true today, when the number of grants, prizes, kudos large and small seems slightly out of control. Who hasn't indulged in the kind of gossip mongering that begins, "Well, you know why/how he/she got it?" Too often, one's own merit is merited, and the merit of others, meretricious. Nevertheless, should one find a peer extolling the crucialness of influence, he or she runs the risk of being judged fulsome. Artists guard the myth of rugged individualism more closely than any other rugged group, sometimes defensively invoking underexposure: "What I haven't read or seen cannot have influenced me." This mistakes the nature of influence, which is not synonymous with primogeniture; lineage can take circuitous routes. If you haven't read Rousseau, you've still gotten him through osmosis.

Originality is always contingent, not simply on one's artistic mentors. In any case, to fully acknowledge one's mentor requires a healthy cap on one's sense of anxiety about the inherited measure of one's powers.

Mentorship requires some degree of acumen or achievement on the part of the acolyte, the mentored, the mentee. In a sense, this means that mentorship can never be completely acknowledged or fully comprehended when the apprenticeship is being served. It makes no aesthetic sense for one to have had a mentor in an enterprise one went on to fail, or one which evaporated through a prolonged penury of success. In other words, mentoring is as much a remembered, more precisely an eidetic function, as it is an actual relationship.

It is in the nature of teaching that some students will surpass their teachers in their productivity, originality, in the ripples of their own influence. The graceful mentor gives the student his or her due, is proud (and here humility, real or feigned, kicks in) of the role played in the shaping of the once-disciple's intellectual adolescence, and can accept a duly measured echo of the importance of their own work. Lisette Model's relationship with Diane Arbus (though not without a small measure of ambivalence) comes to mind.

In the essay "Fires," in the book of the same name, Raymond Carver discusses many of the parameters of influence memorably. He speaks about his dominant influences with a candor that infuriated some people—not in the unexpected twist at the beginning, in which Carver pushes the idea of literary mentorship from the question of stylistics to a more general and inspirational genealogy, noting that Durrell and not Hemingway was responsible for his aesthetic fire, but rather in the situation of having children in his late teens. Carver insists, with a kind of negative dialectic, that the problem of juvenile fatherhood was a nearly insurmountable writing block when he was young and admits that if he had it to do over again, he wouldn't, counseling the same for other young writers. The complaints were a sentimental tyrannizing of memory: one simply *must* look back on the experience of child raising with gratitude and good humor, no matter what. The critics believed he was being unkind, especially to his son, from whom Carver admitted he was somewhat estranged. The real churlishness, though, was in the refusal to accept an unsentimental vision of the past. This is how I feel when I'm asked about my divorce. Much of the time, I get an automatic response that because it produced my son, whom I adore, I have to be grateful that I had an unhappy marriage. I find this kind of argument perverse.

Carver also speaks of the early help and encouragement John Gardner had given him, when they were student and teacher at Humboldt State. Gardner only had a few years on Carver, but he was there, there where Carver wanted to be, and where, ironically, almost tragically, Gardner came to feel Carver had arrived, displacing him, though not directly. Carver's essay is helpful in reminding us of some of the parameters of mentorship, a more wide-ranging term than its comparatively recent retreat to the limitations of academic mentorhood suggests. Lord Chesterfield helped us down that road with his epistolary advice to his son: "Seek the friendly care and assistance of your

Mentor." Paternalistic to the core, part mentor, part Polonius to succeeding generations, Chesterfield gracefully pushed for his own surrogate.

Ray Carver was my teacher, and a generous, lovely one. I remember his economical classes: Ray Carver short stories of classes. They were supposed to be three hours, but we were out in one, because Ray insisted on precision, in our responses, and gave us his in return. He would send me funny postcards cards after I moved to Texas from Syracuse, where I studied with him.

As for other some other mentor substitutes, Spencer saw mentorship in "Reflection's mentor-frown," a superegoish image, the internalization of influence. Byron, in "The Island," describes the sea as "The deep . . . the only Mentor he had known." Between Spencer and Chesterfield and Byron, at least, mentors could run silent or deep, affectionately, reflectively, or fathomlessly. We are mentored by what we need, or contemplate, or see already, Narcisssus-like, in watery looking glasses.

~~~

It is hard to invoke myths of mentorship in our culture without some consideration of movies—our primary myth apparatus—and their mentors: *A Star Is Born* presents the mentor-lover-husband-father as the falling star to the shooting star of his mentored wife. When I was young, Mister Chips, of *Goodbye* fame, that sentimental Mentor for All Seasons, especially as played by Robert Donat in the movie, still had a thread of kitschy dignity. He was swept aside by the suspicious astringency of Miss Jean Brodie's more complex persona. These were mentors to groups, generally, perhaps as much as individually inspiring, and as such they may argue against some of what I've said.

Movie mentors these days are either otherworldly—Yoda, who is also quite worldly (more three-dimensional than old Chips); E.T., the transcendent mentor as innocent (a child shall lead them); the Terminator, the mechanical mentor clone of *Terminator 2*—or more conventionally Other, such as the traditional Confucian-type orientalism of Mister Miyagi in the *Karate Kid* and that of the *Kung Fu Panda* movies. The number of nontraditional mentors devoted to a variety of martial skills gives one pause. One of my favorite variations of this sub-subgenre is *Terminator 2*: the mentor as inhuman killing machine with a sensitive side. I also like Sonny Chiba's Hattori Hannzo in *Kill Bill*: the mentor who needs to occasionally beat his acolyte into submission. Some of the above have the remains of the day of the guru, the fad of spiritual advising that seems to have wafted into our culture in a vague way as traditional religion has slipped among a certain demographic. But do I speak too fast? Were not the Dionne Warwick–led astrological infomercials (dial 1-900-MENTOR?), the spooky attention given to apocalyptic pronouncements, a resurgence in the search for the Great Mentor? A mentor is supposed to show us the way, so it was, and is, a small leap to a yearning for the Mentor to show us The Way. The predicatory can yield to the predatory. Koresh, Jim Jones, Sun Yung Moon, Ronald Reagan. Robert Bly ("Iron Man Mentor"?), Goddess worship (Women Who Run with Mentors?), How to Be Your Own Best Mentor? Chicken Soup for the Unmentored Soul?

The eighties gave us James Olmos in *Stand and Deliver* and Robin Williams in *Dead Poets Society*. Both rely crucially on the possibility of failure, even death, to attempt to hype the necessity for their superteachers, the only master-mentors who can win what is otherwise a losing battle. These archetypes are metaphors for the beginning of the shrunken status of teachers, and they are also symbols of our yearning for them. Now, the mentors on screen tend to be coaches. Lots of coaches. Paul Giamatti, that locker-room world is not really where I find my inspiration.

The desire for direction, for wisdom, precisely when we have, with so much resistance, uncovered the Achilles' heel of authority, uncovers new possibilities for mentoring, but it also puts us at an initiate's disadvantage when we act like tyromaniacs, shooting down the authority we seek. What if there were no author(ity)? Could we pay homage to the authoritative text? Birthless, deathless, inscrutable, an illusion of communication as we have conceived of it? Or perhaps we can join with Strether from James's *The Ambassadors*, in one of my favorite mentoring moments in literature. Strether tells little Bilham, in Gloriani's garden, "Live all you can; it's a mistake not to. . . . One has the illusion of freedom; therefore don't be, like me, without the memory of that illusion. . . . Don't at any rate miss things out of stupidity." Mentoring, and being mentored, is the directed use of the experience of experience, in whatever form it takes. Of course, Strether is ironically being taught by youth as well as trying to tell it what, perhaps, it can never know and what he has just learned. Mentoring, of course, does require the novice, needs it for its own purposes. At its best we think of this as mutual, a platonic exchange of gifts. God knows I've learned enormously from my students. At its worst it can be parasitic, whether parasite or host is the bigger problem. The need for applause and the need for instruction both have their pathological possibilities.

Mentors gone astray: one is tempted to call the victims dementored. Or is it time to enshrine the antimentor, the Mephistophelean provocateur? Think of Dracula, that Satan-mentor derivative, who teaches the love bite and the trick of the kill;

Frankenstein's creature, the student-son-monster ("What have I created!") is ill nurtured, hence ill-natured, id-struck, and out of control, and is also a parental myth, a myth of psychological projection and Prometheanism. In the movie versions, Bela Lugosi and Boris Karloff are the two most dramatic examples of the cause and effect of maniacal mentoring. Of course Satan himself is the greatest antimentor of them all: didn't he teach us everything?

How strange, in this mentorial meditation, to almost end with the movies: they continue to lurk around the edges of my greatest interest, threatening to trample my human mentors, to push my books off their shelves like some kinetic daemon, creeping into memory like insinuations. Memory, that unreliable narrator, is the ultimate auteur of experience. And if it is in memory that we find our mentors, it is the very instability of any autobiographical project that puts a spin on our greatest influences, that makes of them icons with the potential of casting long shadows or crumbling as we recast a self that wants to break the mold. Perhaps in five years, James Agee will have been my primary mentor, my main man. Pauline Kael? Preston Sturges? Alfred Hitchcock? John Garfield? Edward Everett Horton?

THE ART OF SURVIVAL

ON DATING

Like many people my age, after a few forays into dating in high school, my social life became a kind of "falling into" with more and less significant others. I spent a lot of time in schools and academic settings, time in cities and in college towns, and you were around people, and if you and they were available, you kissed in dark corners, or lived together for several years, or fucked and battled until you exhausted each other psychically and moved on, or dallied and flitted about . . . but you didn't exactly "date" in the conventional sense. You didn't participate in that social ritual of calling and meeting up with someone you didn't really know, fumbling around with your social self, your ego, your desires, which our culture depends on for a large part of its mating ritual. I was always grateful: it seemed like something exotic birds or squirrels did, that severe checking out of potential partners. But I was also a bit curious. And postmarried, if predivorced, in a new city, I was wanted to meet someone, create some kind of intimate connection. I was bored and lonely, and I've never liked being alone, never bought the whole solitary life as good for the soul ideology. I like being partnered, like the dialectic, the friction of two people together. There have been times in my life when, fairly obviously in retrospect,

I've stayed disastrously partnered rather than be alone. Oh, call me irresponsible! But anyone who has been alone for long enough inside of a marriage understands the pent-up desire to explore the world of available boys or girls when the curtain falls on the girl or boy one has gone kaput with.

I hooked up with a couple of the online services, since that is apparently the only way anyone meets anyone now: Match and JDate (I thought it might be interesting to go out with a Jewish woman again after a thirty-five-year gap, even if my own ironic sense of identity made me a bit queasy: CurlyNeurotics.com? KvetchandKiss? NeveronaSaturday? . . . I had my own euphemisms . . .) were my preferred imaginary organs. Let that go. The idea of my family's projected joy was startling, nauseating, somewhat horrifying, though. I started dating while I was still married, still cohabiting, a route that was, I understand, not the path many would take. I was, however, not exactly emotionally pining for a marriage that had any green left in its leaves; I had just a few friends and was switching off nights on childcare. I was spending a lot of time at the movies. I'm willing to see almost anything, anytime. Want to drag me to a camp horror film? Not my *primo* genre, but ok. Certainly any noir, any musical, anything Warner Brothers, obscure melodramas, Almodovar, Korean film festival, celebration of the oeuvre of Roddy McDowall—I don't care. I'll run out to see the new Aki Kaurismäki, and if you even want to grab a coffee and talk about James Gleason, give me a call. *J'aime la vie cinematique!*

But even so, to paraphrase Groucho Marx, I like to take myself out of the theater once in a while. And I started using dating as almost a kind of hobby and as an emotional distraction for the turmoil of a divorce that I came to call The Divorciad.

I'm going to tell you a story, of course. And it will be funny. Anecdotes are like essay candy. They're your reward for listening to me, to the essayist, talk. But I'm always a bit fraught when it comes to narrative. There is no denying the illustrative power of story and our primitive desire for it. Of course, stories themselves aren't usually what interest me most. What most engage me are questions, extrapolations from experience, ideas that shake the warp and woof of my experiential bearings. But autobiographical narratives have also served me as fodder and as the building blocks for extending speculations on what I think I'm doing in the world, how I think I'm generally misconceiving things, which I think is a generally more interesting path than trying to prove why your equation is sound math.

One of the things I gathered early on in my dating escapade (which makes the whole thing sound more madcap than it was, as though I was some Max Sennett character crashing through the window of a sushi bar) was how deeply the years of attending to myself—for example writing essays, exploring the nature of my selves through time in linked narratives—had affected my presentation of self. I was somewhat taken aback to find, with Lamb, "how art thou changed, Thou art sophisticated!" I was smooth and controlled—somewhat polished even—in my social demeanor. I was extremely effective at establishing a kind of intimacy very quickly, partly by asking questions and gently probing, partly by what I chose to reveal, and partly through tone, which was warm. Let's say an oboe. All of this was very revealing when my self-image, the last time I had dated, had hovered somewhere between Eddie Bracken in *Miracle of Morgan's Creek*, Lou Costello, and Leo Gorcey.

I have to stop here and elaborate more, because I realize I'm in danger of sounding like some kind of dating lounge lizard. I don't mean that at all. I mean, instead, that after years of writing essays, talking about autobiography, years, in fact, of being in therapy, of adapting a largely psychoanalytic way of considering most situations, years of second guessing myself, considering and reconsidering my motives, playing with the language of memory, trying to understand the implications of it and the metaphors we use to consider it, years of thinking about myself in rooms full of strangers, backing myself into corners, literally and figuratively, as I overthought the painful complexity of saying hello to someone I didn't know, years of talking to students about their most revealing and painful experiences and how they might render them, how they might honor them, how they might, if the circumstances fit, go at them like a mad dog, years of walking down streets by myself at night (looking in clothing store windows, shops of bric-a-brac), thinking that making a fundamentally beautiful and lasting connection with a partner was impossible on the level of charged trusting connection that I wanted, as though what I was looking for were just short of incest, a kind of sibling-like playful supersexual, utterly trusting, joined-at-the-hip-across-a-crowded-room thing that still didn't involve some kind of nasty mirroring of the self because who wants to have that ding! ding! sensation with themselves, I mean, as if you couldn't tell, I like my company, but I get awfully, awfully, awfully tired of myself sometimes. So, what I mean to say is that by the time I started dating, I could communicate my sense of self clearly and vividly to the person opposite me. I was used to drawing other people out. And I had a well-developed affective vocabulary. This is all to say, women—those who didn't find me too short (who were churlish creatures from the outset)—tended to like me fairly well.

One thing that hasn't changed much about me over time is that I prefer to be somewhat passive when it comes to my initial interchanges with women in any kind of mating ritual. While I couldn't go out with everyone who contacted me (the twenty-two-year-old in West Germany was an avid chess and beach volleyball player, and I'm not that big on chess), I did go out with a lot of women. And I did have some reasonably odd experiences.

One woman who seemed very interesting was a Jewish high school Latin teacher. She taught at a large Chicago Catholic high school, and I was really intrigued by what her cultural milieu was like and how she pulled it off. I spent my childhood in the suburb of Our Lady of Grace, in Brooklyn, and a part of me has always looked over the cultural fence. The wife I was Homerically divorcing (Note, Goddess, the price of attorneys) was Catholic, at least on Easter, after we separated, until the 5 p.m. transition. I thought my date might be like some undercover Jew, some Jew in duress. I had visions, before the date, of taking communion with her, after a drink or two. You know, she would show up to work in some Jewish trench coat that hid the Jewishness underneath. All day long she was afraid her Jewishness would show. But her superb Latin kept her safe, as long as no one, no jealous yenta from the Jewish Community Center, made an anonymous call to the principal saying, "There is a stranger among you." That sort of thing. She was a pleasantly attractive woman, very thin, almost a kind of wastrel, really—wan, with soulful, slightly mad eyes that seemed to be looking inward, searching for something unsurely. After some pleasant conversation at the bar of an Italian restaurant, she asked if she could hold my hand. She smiled sweetly at me, in a way that was genuine, endearing, kind of nuts. I thought she was interesting, and since I was halfway through my second Gibson, I agreed. Her name was Charna. I seemed to remember we spoke about declensions and dogs; she said her entire neighborhood hated her dog, and she didn't know why. The dog had nearly bit another dog once, but it was all a big mistake. I had a cousin in Queens who had had a similar mishap. I spoke a bit about moving to Chicago, a bit about My Situation. It seems interesting now, looking back, how unconcerned most women were about the fact that I was cohabiting with the wife I was separated from and in divorce proceedings with. I can't say, in similar circumstances, I would find that very reassuring. I was a bit like a teenager who could never take a date home because he had a deranged mother sitting in the living room, knitting. I'm not sure what to make of that, other than that perhaps I was very convincingly separated, that I was taken as trustworthy and sincere about the finality of my marriage, emotionally, and that logistically, the legal part would end (Bellow, Goddess . . .) before, I thought, the next cicada life cycle had run its course.

Sincerity is an interesting quality to talk about, to isolate, both in nonfiction writing and in person. It's quite different, after all, from honesty, even from trustworthiness. Conventionally, I think, we understand sincerity to mean conveying truth of feeling, genuineness in conveying what the speaker or writer believes or thinks. We feel we are being spoken to in the moment, without duplicity, when we experience sincerity. But sincerity can be complicated by self-deception and time. We've all had the experience of (Have we? Haven't we? Do I overgeneralize?) passionately or hypercritically arguing a point as though there were virtually no other way to see it, think it, feel it, only to find ourselves later, having had the graceful experience of actually listening to someone else and realizing that our position, our thoughts, our feelings weren't the white hot lightning rod of truth they seemed in the moment . . . a sincere but flawed line of reasoning, something we now wanted to disown. Again, sincerely. Sincerity and trustworthiness can also be mimed, of course. Or so fleeting as to be virtually useless. It is as a longer term extension of character, or over the course of a body of work, that we get a clearer idea of a person's, a writer's sincerity as a deeper quality, as a part of ethos and not of tone. Sincerity as tone is how one appears over a drink, what one might reveal in a paragraph. Sincerity as character, as ethos, is the ability to construct a consistently trustworthy self over the course of multiple works or in a relationship in its many forms.

That was about as eventful as the night got. I dropped Charna off and bid her adieu with a chaste tap on the cheek. She called me up a few days later and asked me to go to dinner and a movie. She was lovely and sincere, after all, despite being somewhat overzealous. If she were grabbing at men's hands impulsively, and not just mine, and considering my need for engagement that didn't cost $400.00 an hour (I'm talking about attorneys, not women who are paid to hold hands), that didn't seem a far stretch. But our second date was inauspicious. She had the sniffles and, over a bowl of excellent Vietnamese consommé at Tank Noodle, asked me to skip the movie and come back to her place to meet her dog, which I agreed to innocently, having nothing else to do, though conversation had lagged at dinner, both of us seeming to find the other a bit elusive. I've often wondered about the nature of this invitation, if it were actually some kind of euphemism that slipped by me years ago: "Come back to my place and, you know, 'meet the dog.'" "Hey, Dave, did you 'meet the dog'?" "Hey, fellas, what a night. You know, I 'met the dog.'" I don't know. If it is, it's obscure, or some Latin translation from the Hebrew, some idiomatic blip or something. I thought that when I lived in England and got "put the kettle on," I was all set. In any case, we did go back to her place, and I did meet the dog that the neighbor hated. It was a very big dog that didn't bark so much as moan in a singsongy way when you got close to it. It made me a bit sad. The first thing Charna did, after dogs and humans were introduced all around was open the sliding closet doors to show me the cats, and then close the sliding closet doors. I'm not sure why there were cats in the closet. Nor do I think this was in any way a symbolic gesture.

Charna sat on the couch, and I sat on a chair. And we had a feeble conversation—I don't remember about what. She seemed to grow progressively sadder and more distracted, and I grew increasingly bemused by exactly what I was doing—I really didn't have a clue, or rather I was clearly not terribly interested in Charna at this point, though I wasn't at all unhappy about sitting there, somewhat disengaged from any real social involvement and considering her furniture and her, considering myself and what a general idiot I was in so many ways, how odd, disastrous, unpredictable, and lonely my life had been, despite lovely friends' relationships. It's nightmarish to think that the thing that saves me from moments of despair—sitting in a slightly shabby apartment in Chicago at the age of fifty in the middle of (Pipe down, Goddess . . .) a divorce during a date that was veering toward a combination of David Lynch and Pee-wee Herman—is the ability to stop and pull inside, to try to be the person on whom nothing is lost, to look around and see where I am and how I'm situated, which is also the reason for where I am and how I'm situated. In other words, the reason I was OK in this crazy situation and am now spinning out what may or may not be an entertaining paragraph about it is what put me there in the first place: a kind of adaptable interest in the world and seeing myself in it. I'm terribly polite and very adaptable socially because there is such a well-carved self inside, a self that started taking notes when I was twelve or so because it needed a bit of distance, some ballast from the unkindness of the world, which never seemed to fail to point out how weak, how gross, how underachieving I was. As much as I feel generally like a Montaignian, in this respect I suppose I'm Baconian. I keep my counsel, even when I play the neurotically revealing

Jewish New Yorker. Though, I also have a deep desire for revelation, honesty, and trust. I am speaking about moments that are liminal, times when I am in the gray areas of real intimacy, mock intimacy, trial intimacy, public gatherings, and new acquaintances.

And the reason I write essays is to try to find moments, sincerely, when I press myself, press the advantage of my own controls to the point where I learn something a little bit new. For instance, I think my politeness, which I've always thought of as a bit Old Worldy, is useful to me, in a limited way. It gives me pleasure, for one thing, because it's attached to gestures and language ("I beg your pardon"; "It would be my pleasure"; "You're too kind"; "It was a lovely evening, and it was charming of you to have me") that I associate with an earlier age, with my parents, with the films of the thirties and forties, with phrases heard in elevators in Manhattan as a child. I'm dating myself. But my politeness is also a kind of courtly persona that I can adopt with a well-used ease at this point. It isn't that I'm not being genuine when I'm being polite (or is it?), but that I'm conveying an attitude more than something personal. Though, it's a sincere attitude.

In any case, at Charna's apartment, I was reasonably comfortable in an uncomfortable situation because I didn't want or need anything particularly more than what I had at the moment—a place to sit and think, and she perhaps had more pressing needs: a greater intimacy, a fine romance, opening and shutting the closet with cats—I cannot speak for her and should not. But after some *longeurs*, which seemed long even to me, she announced, "I'm going to walk the dog, and then the date will be over." Reader, do you do internal double takes? I said, "That's fine," and began to parse the sentence. It was clear she was ending the evening, now that the canine introduction, euphemistic or not, had been performed and had turned into a desultory affair, and I felt dismissed, the way you feel you have been less than amusing, less than ingratiating, less than sincere, in the presence of someone you had been observing, perhaps even tolerating. That Charna's end of the night signal (I was sure that "walking the dog" was not another euphemism) was absurd made the acknowledgment that she was no more interested in me than I was authentically so in her an excellent, mirroring reminder that the years I spent achieving a measure of social equanimity, which is to say the ability to exist in a state of relative ease in a social situation in which I wasn't completely comfortable without the compelling desire to sprint for the nearest elevator or window, didn't relieve me of the need for empathy.

Am I being empathetic to Charna even now? Or is she just a foil for my quixotic, ever-present need to pull myself, my own motives apart. At what point does the desire for self-knowledge actually slide into something more narcissistic. Charna: I chose a satirical name for her, Hebraically dark, or burnt, the narrative sacrifice to . . . what? My need to amuse, to rope in the reader with something entertaining to wrap around the notions of the remembering self? Lazar, my own name, has ancient etymological connections to blackness. Is this my subconscious connection to self-mockery. My unconscious connection to . . . connection?

We all know that the motions of confession can be as canned, as predictable, as epiphanies. And that sincerity is a fraught, even a dialectical quality. Public sincerity is not necessarily private sincerity, and we may, in fact, as post-Rousseaueans, be relying on our private selves as keepers of the most sincere part of ourselves, or the realest sense of sincerity we experience. What if the ubiquity of the public self has forced sincerity into a corner, where no one can see it? What if we feel that the persona that's really real is, by definition, the one that can never be seen, never be corrupted by a hall of mirrors? Trilling, of course, has much to say in *Sincerity and Authenticity* (which was required reading when I was in college) about the growth of autobiographical works of literature and the development of the sincere self and its replacement by a struggle for authenticity. Inspired, no doubt, by Montaigne's sincerity ("My imperfections will be seen here to the life") ("To the Reader"), Hamlet says, "To thine own self be true," the aphoristic commandment of sincerity, one would think. But as Arthur Melzer suggests in "Rousseau and the Modern Cult of Sincerity" (Harvard Review, Spring, 1995), sincerity may have devolved into a quality of self-disclosure, "an adherence to the self" that eschews other qualities, such as honesty, truth, or plainspokenness.

I don't want you think I felt terrible that night or that I'm feeling now some self-lacerating guilt. That would be insincere. But I think it wise to question, considering the depth of my observing self, the relationship between the observing selves I live, the observing selves I remember, and the observing selves I write. Untangling them is impossible. And wise, too, to look at the nature of self-disclosure—the way, for example, I began dating (Shhhh, Goddess . . .): I did so within the limits of decorum, so naturally, so sincerely, but with an edge of performative skill. I've spoken enough to and about the self over the years not to be able to put mine over with some alacrity, I think. It is a dangerous quality, because it creates a false, or shall we say an intensified, sense of intimacy. Do I talk about myself too easily now? This can be a problem when meeting people you have no desire to ever see again, to whom self-revelation creates expectancy, intimacy. And it should. And in fact, in the rest of my life, it does. But it was strange to see that what had become one of my self's processes, one of my habits of being, to paraphrase

Flannery O'Connor, had also become, or was in danger of becoming, a tic, a habit performed without sufficient due process of empathetic concern. Look, it isn't as though I were talking to a mirror or that my interest in my companions for the evening were feigned. It's just that as I did my analyst/analysand number at this or that bar or this or that restaurant, what I probably wanted most was for someone to find me fascinating and irresistible, and self-disclosure was my instrument. And I'm sure everything I said, or almost everything, was sincere. Speaking about myself falsely is like being made to eat a food I've cooked and detest. I don't really see the point. Why bother creating a false idol of oneself, since you know you're going to have to throw the tablets down at some point anyhow?

You may wonder why I didn't just try more assiduously to make friends in the months of painful cohabitation. You may wonder why I didn't just buckle down and spend the time more usefully alone. You may wonder how I could spend so many nights rehearsing myself with different women, presenting the self, presenting myself in semihopefulness that some connection might be made, only to hear to the vague hissing of air escaping. You may wonder how anyone can begin the process of courting while one's marriage is in the process of legal dissolution. Some of these questions are worth essays of their own; some will be dispatched by certain readers with knowing recognition. I'll just say that my own—choose your frame of reference for this moment in this essay—set of needs, neurotic make-up, sense of situational necessity, emotional philosophy or pathology or ideology seems to just about demand the idea of romantic love, the sometimes labyrinthine or perverse pursuit of coupling. Blame it on Fred and Ginger, blame it on the family, blame it on the troubadours, or blame it on a fleeting glimpse of a couple walking in Central Park on a fall day from our family's Buick in 1965. They were wearing lamb's wool sweaters and jeans, holding hands, and talking. I think they were talking to each other about themselves. Both had glasses. Is that why I can't seem to stop talking about myself, writing about myself?

Is every essay I write a date, and is the date really with myself?

DEATH, DEATH, DEATH, DEATH, DEATH

It is life which is the Great Unknown

E. M. CIORAN, *A Short History of Decay*

My mother has become a kind of painful signifier of her own absence in the years since she died, a symbol of the way a wound effaces the cut while not healing. She died when I was in my early twenties, starting to reconcile with her, after years of self-imposed emotional exile. This, what felt like diabolical intervention, has haunted much of my life and left me with a permanently acute appreciation for ironic near misses, almost happeneds, and slight fluctuations in the warps and woofs of circumstance. In short, I think I have come to appreciate, shall we say, in not always the healthiest of ways, how circumstance is connected to loss and how it is inscribed commonly, frequently, frequently painfully as an ironic marker of the Big Loss behind me, and ahead of me.

I was talking awhile back to a writer friend who said that she didn't think coincidence was an interesting category of experience to write about. I was struck by this (one is usually struck, in fact, by coincidence), since sometimes I think it is the only thing interesting worth writing about. Oh, not in a mystified woo-woo kind of way, as in some guiding spirit outside ourselves leading the co's toward incidence. But in the sense that we manage to find delightful surprises and combinations, strange pairings and meetings, and then are forced to do the work that is our continuing important work: finding meaning in experience. Everything means something, after all. Even nihilists have an ideological template.

When I fell on the ice this winter, I was more or less in the same position my mother was in when she died. Arms at my side. A woman walking by never breaking her stride said, "Are you all right be careful." And I immediately thought, "Horse is out of the fucking barn on that one, honey." I had a huge hematoma on the right side of my head. I had been distracted that morning, because I had woken up with a lump on my chest, surrounded by a large area of internal bleeding. And I was rushing to meet my divorce lawyer. My hands were in my pockets. My hands always seem to be in my pockets, some internal huddling mechanism. But everybody in Brooklyn knows it's stupid to walk on the ice with your hands in your pockets. No way to break the fall. I wasn't all right, and I wasn't careful. The lump turned out to be a benign cyst. The bleeding was oh so mysterioso. The concussion still gives me atypical migraines on the right side of my head to go with the atypical migraines on the left side of my head from the car accident I was in after my last relationship. "Every day a little death . . . in the heart and in the head" (Stephen Sondheim).

Today is the fortieth anniversary of the death of Robert Kennedy. He was the first politician I fell in love with. There was a string after him, whom I worked for: McGovern, Bella Abzug,

Ramsey Clark. I wish I were in love again. I don't think I'm capable of it anymore. But Bobbie was the first. My brother and I pleaded with my mother to vote for him. I remember watching a press conference in the living room and waiting on my mother's response; she had told us she would if he answered a certain way about Israel. Apparently he did, and she said, OK, she would, and we said, hooray. And then the Ambassador. There is something differently sad, pathetic really, about a child's presidential hero being assassinated. It's something like the introduction of death into a political family romance. The next month, my family traveled to California. As though paying subconscious homage to the loss of innocence, we went to Disneyland and stayed at the Ambassador. Walking back to the hotel one evening, I ran ahead to a newsstand to get a paper. (We always had newspapers around. If I can lose myself in a newspaper, my anxieties, existential or petty, tend to diminish.) Soviet tanks had gone into Czechoslovakia. Back at the hotel, I stole an ashtray from the lobby and wrote "Bobby" on it in Magic Marker when we got home.

Bo Diddley died yesterday. "Who Do You Love." I love my son. A ragtag group of friends in places that look like an idiot was throwing darts at a map. It would be fun to start naming them. Like an Oscar speech. I wonder which ones would be embarrassed, and which, amused. I love the younger me, that boy who needed his mother's love so fiercely. As Charles Lamb reminds us, we need to take care of our younger selves. How they can be tended, it seems to me, is various. They may need befriending, or they may need foster parentage. But they simply cannot take care of themselves.

My grandparents lived downstairs, in the lower apartment of our row house in Brooklyn, when I was growing up. My grandfather died when I was eight. I remember being taken to the office at school because my father was there; if you hadn't been a bad child, that meant someone was dead. It was a kind of minor celebrity to go home from school in the middle of the day. I remember being pleased and sad, feeling queasy because I felt kind of excited about being pulled out of school. I felt guilty. Of course, it didn't take much. I was breathing. My memories of my grandfather define fondness, define the benign. I remember him rowing me around a lake in the Catskills, his strong, old, tanned body and Russo-Siberian face. He didn't say much, but spoke with a gently firm authority, a thick and deep, melodically accented English. I remember eating herring with him in his kitchen. But I don't remember too much else. And he essentially lived with us. And I was eight when he died. Neurotic that I am, this has translated to how many years I need to live to have my son accumulate significant memory of me before I die. If he gets pulled out of school, I want him to feel deeply wounded, though not traumatized.

Next year, I will be my mother's age when she died of lung cancer. I smoked for many years. Every day, etc.

When I was hired at Ohio University, where I taught for many years, my chair was a man who, nearing retirement, died suddenly. By suddenly, I mean he didn't feel well on Friday and was dead on Sunday. At his funeral, a friend went for some water and came back and told me not to look in the room with the open door. Really, he said, don't do it. Right. As though if this happened to you, you'd say, "Oh, OK, you bet I won't!" So I went for some water and peaked in the open door, and I had to keep looking to figure out what I was seeing. Clearly, some things could be reasonably established with alacrity, such as (*a*) this was a room; (*b*) the door was open; (*c*) there was a coffin in a corner of the room; (*d*) there was absolutely nothing else in the room, including chairs, table, etc.; (*e*) in the coffin was a body; (*f*) the body was dark skinned. But things became problematic at this point, because the head of the body looked to be two or three times the size of a normal head and didn't look real. It looked like a big, brown doll head. And it was hard to determine gender because of the grotesqueness, and I was . . . I was loathe to get closer to this death-thing. I returned to my friend and simply blurted out to him, "Holy Christ, it's Old Mother Death." She reappeared in our conversations over the years, as a kind of totem, a reminder to invoke the darkness before it creeps up on you. But I'm hardly unaware of: "old," "mother," "death."

I knew seven kids who died in high school. One fell in between the subway cars. One was stabbed to death. One was a very dear girl whom I had known since second grade—Lisa Septoff. I had had a terrible crush on her. We separated in junior high, off to different schools, but used to meet on the bicycle path on Ocean Parkway and ride together. She was hit by a car while riding her bike and died instantly. Three popular girls from my high school who worked at a hotel upstate were killed in a fire there. It was on the front page of the *Daily News*—that's how I found out about it. One of the girls sat in front of me in our alphabetized homeroom. The teacher called her Meyer Lansky. Phillip Bernstein overdosed and drowned in a swimming pool in Florida. In our yearbook, there's a photo of him smiling and leaning on my shoulder. He was a really sweet guy. I always thought he gave drugs a good name.

I remember writing on "Out of the Cradle Endless Rocking" for my comprehensive exams, and the only line I could remember verbatim (which I do not forget) was "Death, death, death, death, death." I passed.

Richard Selzer told me that he still dreams about smoking all the time, even after having quit years ago, having had a collapsed lung. He said that if he gets a terminal diagnosis, the first thing he's going to do is go out and buy a pack of cigarettes.

I was spending an afternoon with M. F. K. Fisher, and she heard someone say she was going to kill time. She became furious. "Killing time is an expression I abhor," she told me. "No one should kill time. There isn't enough of it, for one thing. And of course, you can't anyhow." She had advanced Parkinson's disease. And although she was still completely sharp intellectually, she would go into full Parkinsonian freezes, bodily fugue states that would last between twenty minutes and two or three hours.

One of my ways of keeping my constant mortal fears at bay (reminder: check out etymology of "keeping at bay," and checking out etymologies, derivations, the everyday digressions of mortal distraction is one of the essential ways of keeping my constant mortal fears at bay) is to read the *New York Times*. I started reading the *Times* when I was morbidly young. I like using the word "morbidly," which is a deathly term, but also a neurotic one. If the Freudian shoe fits. I was on a date recently and described myself as "morbidly punctual." What did I mean by that? I'm not even quite sure, but aside from the playfulness, and even perverse pride, I think I was implying an obsessiveness bordering on fear, a fear linked to death, that if I were late, I would put my life in peril. Late to my own funeral? No, that if I were late, it would lead to my own funeral. That being on time keeps me alive? In any case (digression is escapism, keeps the angel of death at bay), I started reading the *Times* when I was eight or so, and when I'm in the *Times*, I feel safe, feel like I'm in a world that's familiar and ironically calm, even if reading about the most calamitous events, the most morbid deaths or disasters, writ small or large: tsunamis or self-immolations, crane collapses or just plain men and women collapsing. I'm in there, reading; my eyes are moving; I still have the op-eds, or the Yankees, movie reviews, the obits, especially the obits (hey, I'm not dead—but I don't like it, get queasy if anyone dies too close to my age, which has gotten more ticklish as I've entered my fifties). When I go out to work, as I've done much of my life, grading papers, starting essays or prose poems, messing about with almost but not quite working, I always try to get the *Times* to start off with, to soothe my daily anxiety about starting the day. Starting the day in a world not my own, in which I'm not dead or dying.

I think my father may outlive me. I'm fifty-one and he's eighty-nine. He's stumbled a little healthwise this year: a stent. A fall required a bunch of stitches in his hand. A bad staph infection from some skin cancer surgery. But he pulls through it all fine and goes back to playing golf and going to the theater. I've had my own health problems. The concussion. A hernia surgery. But you don't need to know everything. But I feel sometimes as though I'm in what Spalding Gray called "the Bermuda Triangle" of health. This is the period in your early fifties when you seem to disappear into a sea of assorted health problems. Then, according to Gray, you emerge and live a nice long life. Or you don't.

Ever since I was a boy, the family was organized around the concept of inheritance. The patrilineal pot of gold. It was a subtle form of control and a well-meaning promise at the same time. Negative capability with a positive balance. Nothing that one should live one's live about, and I don't think I have. But the other day, I caught myself thinking, "It's going to skip me and go to my son," and thought up a new psychological category: Princecharlesism, the feeling that death is going to give to a succeeding generation what one had thought one was going to receive or enjoy in one's own life.

Along somewhat similar lines, a friend of mine should be dead by now, because he has been laughing at his liver for thirty-five years, causing great distress to everyone he knows. There have been interventions, etc. I went to his apartment a couple of years ago to surprise him on New Year's Eve, and he threw me out when I mentioned booze. It's some kind of Ripley's thing. Everyone is surprised by his body's willfulness. Apparently his liver is in fine shape, though his brain is beginning to shrink. If he outlives me, it will be another notch in the belt for the Great Imaginary Ironist. It's sometimes very difficult being a nonpracticing, superstitious Jewish atheist who believes that irony is the governing law of the universe. One of my favorite moments in literature is in Lamb's "New Year's Eve," when Lamb, in a mournful mood, thinking of the year's demise, and therefore his own, speaks of the loss of "irony itself." To miss irony in death. Who could not love such an essayist? Well, it is Lamb, after all. My own sense of irony runs more darkly. Still.

Another poet friend seemed to take excellent care of himself, ran, played basketball, did some motorcycle dirt bike racing thing— all despite being a hemophiliac. He seemed to be cheating, or death defying, and, for friends who knew him in his early thirties, balanced an energetic cheerfulness with a complex and intellection. He had great taste in literature, liked writers with quirky visions. He was something of a Pollyanna, we thought, but it was entirely endearing. Once, on a long car ride together, he asked me about dirty words and sex, how it worked and what women liked, and then whether you had to do what you said. A few years later, when he emerged as a closet alcoholic and depressive, it wasn't just that we greeted the information with a kind of disbelief—at least the alcohol part—but with actual disbelief. We thought he didn't know what real drinking was. Still no one knows what his fractured story adds up to. He came from a religious family, Methodist (I don't understand Protestants; Jews and Catholics I've got a pretty good handle on), and had a brother die young. He suffered through breakdowns and a divorce, antidepressants and reemergences. When it seemed that he might be where he wanted to be, perhaps. Maybe. Having decided to marry a woman he had met in Rome, he died of a blood disease, not directly related to his hemophilia. He wrote a memoir that avoids saying anything too painful. He was forty-one.

My friend Lynda, a poet, died at the beginning of the year, in 1991. She was forty-one also. She was several years older than me. "Older than I" seems too fussy to say sometimes. We were poetry students and great friends together in Houston, and after. She was blossoming, and cut down by cancer. She had moved to New York but had to move back to the Minneapolis area for free health care. I had just gotten my first job as a professor at Ohio University. The last I heard from her was a postcard in which she wrote, "Someday, my dear, we will both escape from the Midwest."

I was in a rather serious car accident twelve years ago, which has left me daily migraine headaches—they're atypical, though, not what you'd think of as classical migraines. They're fluttery pressures across the side and top of my head, exacerbated by stress of any kind (such as thinking that I'm dying of something). I take meds that mostly control these. The first few years, while I tried to find doctors to convince that I wasn't crazy, I self-medicated with Dewar's and martinis. The accident occurred on a curvy rural road in Athens, Ohio. I was reaching for a Leonard Cohen CD that John Gallaher had leant me, and a phantom object crossed my path. It might have been a groundhog or a mole or a Leonard Cohen death wish projected onto the road. I was just ending a most destructive relationship. I swung the car into the right guardrail and, to compensate, apparently pulled hard left. I rolled three times and ended up in a ditch. True, I was not driving at thirty-five miles an hour. I do not remember anything about the accident other than thinking I saw something in the road after I reached for Lenny. To cut to the, as it were, chase—in the ditch, I thought I might be dying. Perhaps paralyzed, but very possibly dying. It is difficult to reconstruct my consciousness. The car was a crumpled mass. My flickering consciousness said to itself, "Go to sleep, go to sleep, don't be awake if you're dying or paralyzed." It was a singular moment in my life: fear of death acting as protective narcosis. Yet when I think back to it now, had I in fact been dying, I would have been willing myself away from pain, perhaps, but into death.

I woke up as a man's voice said, "We're getting you out, Bud."

Cyd Charisse died today, and I'm feeling rather mournful about it. Another Astaire shoe has dropped. Another step stopped. I mark my time, not unusually, by the deaths of celebrities. But I've reached the age where the celebrities are of a certain age to really affect me. I must confess I was a bit oblivious to the death of Kurt Cobain, even though I like Nirvana (which sounds funny to say). It would sound funnier to say I could take or leave Nirvana. But I was in Italy when both Astaire and Sinatra died, strangely enough. I'm killing American icons by drinking red wine and eating pigeon and risotto. The friends I was with, in a little village outside of Florence, called Castelfranco di Sopra, thought I was silly for being so bothered by Astaire's death. They were social scientists. I think they thought I was mourning on the level of, say, Paulo Freire. But the fluid, indefinable masculinity of Astaire, the otherworldly trances of the great dances with Rogers (I clung tenaciously to the two of them as the necessary pair) had been important to me ever since I started watching them on four o'clock movies—my gateway to so much ideological twaddle and necessity, so many images of charming impossibility, tuxes and gowns, beauty and wit, bandstands and banter, art deco and décolletage. And Astaire had never soured, had never become some third-rate embarrassment or first-rate political ideologue, and thus had stayed fresh, despite the occasional late role in dramatic potboilers, in which he still managed to retain his dignity.

É Ginger Dansa Sola, the headline said.

Then Sinatra took a dive when I was in Rome. I overheard a couple at the next table talking about it. As if anyone had died, as in, yeah, Sinatra died. I mean, this was Rome. If the pope had died, you wouldn't say it like that. And who, after all, was really more important, in lasting terms?

Anyhow, today is death day for El Cyd, the most gracefully moving presence in American cinema. *The Band Wagon* is probably my favorite musical, partially because it introduces the pathos of aging Astaire, still moving beautifully, into the picture and hooks him up on that carriage ride in the dark with Cyd, who then dances with him in the park. We all want to ride into the dark with someone who can dance with us, even as the memory of what we once could do starts to fade.

If I were to take a powder now, would this essay be enough? Is it death worthy? Does it hold enough death. Does it carry its death well? If I were cut off midstream of consciousness, would the irony power me through to publication? Would David include the essay in *The Seattle Review*? This is more than a writerly worry, of course. It is the distilled version of what I think about when I go to bed at night. Is it enough? Have I been enough? Can I say one more thing that might at least put something else over to make up for the time I've spent sitting around reading the *Times*, scanning the obits? And writing about death, I think about Spalding Gray . . . well, many things about Gray. But in this context, I think first off about him talking in *Swimming to Cambodia* about how he went up a thousand feet in a helicopter without doors. He says,

> We had no safety belts—but I suddenly had no fear because the camera eroticizes the space! It protects you like Colgate Guard-All. Even if the chopper crashed, at least there would be rushes, right? My friends could show them on New Year's Eve at the Performing Garage.

His verdict is, "something would come of this," which is ultimately a stay against death, a momentary calming of one's existential sense that nothing means anything and that falling out of a helicopter is a stupid way to die. Or that *plotzing* (a Yiddish word meaning "falling on your face," but with darker implications at times, a kind of slapstick death) in the middle of writing an essay might leave you having not accomplished much, so you weave your way around it with comic digressive and attention-calling hand waving, as a way of trying to slow your heartbeat a little or throw a gauntlet at the angel of death you don't believe in. I mean, if you keep writing, you'll eventually die, but what are the odds that it will happen now?

Then, when Spalding Gray died, the mixture of shock and the completely predictable. He had been telling us about his suicide for years, hadn't he? Had he? Look at the poster for *Swimming to Cambodia*. Head half-submerged, no body. All the water imagery in Gray's work—the references to his mother's suicide. But his work was so tenderly self-regarding, too. Suicides, I suppose, are twenty-twenty.

George Carlin died. The only seriously angry voice in mainstream culture willing to consistently challenge what's dead in American life. But even Carlin became commodified. The only way not to would be to risk antagonizing your audience so severely that you put your platform in danger. He was a wonderful writer:

> Because thanks to our fear of death in this country, I won't have to die. I'll "pass away," or I'll "expire," like a magazine subscription. If it happens in the hospital, they'll call it a "terminal episode." The insurance company will refer to it as "negative patient care outcome." And if it's the result of malpractice, they'll say it was a "therapeutic misadventure."

The only problem was that when he said, "Fuck you," to his audience, they loved him.

I suppose at this point in the essay, I have to ask myself what my thinking about death, my thinking and thinking about death, my worry about early death (I know I'm not the first boomer to update my take on my generation, bargaining with Pete Townsend about what "old" is) has done for me, or to me, and where to take it from here. Turning to Montaigne, as I do on a regular basis, I find this in the essay "Impermanence":

> To begin depriving death of its greatest advantage over us . . . let us deprive death of its strangeness, let us frequent it, let us get used to it; let us have nothing more often in mind than death. . . . We do not know where death awaits us; so let us wait for it everywhere. To practice death is to practice freedom.

Hmmm. Nix that; I'm too neurotic, too life clutching. I mean, I worship Montaigne, but the stoic thing ain't going to fly with me. I'm terrified of nonexistence. Death as the mother of beauty is a beautiful but incomplete idea. Death is also the mother of putrefaction. And death is the mother of the death of my mother. Death is therefore Deadmotherdeath. I run away. I will always run away.

My mother has been dead several years longer than I knew her alive. It takes on the dimensions of a demented ball score at some point, the numbers bloated. Twenty-eight to twenty-two. My son's numbers won't be so good. He was born when I was forty-four, and I smoked for many years. When I was young, smoking was like drinking—drowning my sorrows in smoke, in ash. The lungs are less recuperative than other organs. I got so drunk on the death I was inhaling—as homage, as legacy—that all I could do was keep sucking it in.

In the last year of my marriage, we almost rented a condo in Chicago whose backyard was a large cemetery. I went back and forth on it. My once again nonwife wasn't that troubled, since

I was the official holder of all neurotic considerations pertaining to family life. I had to wonder if that would adjust my son, then six, to a healthy proximity to the dead or FUCKING CREEP HIM OUT TOTALLY AND GIVE HIM MAJOR NIGHTMARES. Or whether I was talking about myself. Or whether, liking to stroll through graveyards until and unless I get the heebie jeebies, I was mostly worried about myself. Graveyard in back, the condo was also feet from Lake Michigan. All in all, it was a bit too Rebecca. And how to sell it? Just think, every day will be like Halloween! Even kids get tired of playing dead.

One day about twenty-five years ago—so, about three years or so after my mother died—my father was riding the train with me out to JFK from Manhattan. He was a travel agent who had more or less retired but still had a stake in an agency and knew everybody at Pan Am and TWA and was going to try to get me on a full flight to Italy. He was in midsentence and just stopped as his head slumped down to his chest. "Pop?" I shook him. He was unresponsive. I was sure he was dead. I shook him again. Again. Then he woke up.

> Sense the solving emptiness
> That lies just under all we do,
> . . . .
> So permanent and black and true.

This from "Ambulances," by Philip Larkin. At Larkin's funeral, in 1985, which I attended, sending away for tickets from the Rector of Westminster Abbey (would there be scalping, I wondered?), a pastor intoned about the distress he felt, or felt we might be feeling, for Larkin's disbelieving soul, and he assured us that he would be forgiven. Larkin's always bolstered up my atheistic soul (*sic*), my sometimes sick but usually resolute atheistic soul, when it wanders toward the precipice of false sentimental doubt in my faith in disbelief. Larkin reassures me nothing's there, that despite the swollen crowd walking past the BBC cameras into Westminster, the disturbing beauty of the trombone solo playing "Just a Closer Walk with Thee," despite the sense of great moment in the presence of Chaucer and Ben Jonson, Hardy and Dickens, some are there to observe, and some are under the white sheet. How perfect, or perfectly ironic, as I rose from my folding chair in the South Transept, to realize that I had been sitting on T. S. Eliot's memorial through Philip Larkin's funeral. Eliot's epitaph, from "Little Gidding": "The communication / Of the dead is tongued with fire beyond the language of the living." I felt chastened. But true to the spirit of Larkin, I also noted that my ass has been poised above the communication of the dead for nearly an hour and a half.

I don't have much of a problem with illness as a metaphor. Sontag recanted on much of it, too. Death as a metaphor, however, seems a bit presumptuous. Someone wrote to me recently about a painful emotional situation I'm going through, that it must feel a little like death. Fuck if I know. Of course, I've always interpreted that to mean it feels like dying. Does it mean it feels like experiencing the death of someone else? Occasionally, I learn that I've misunderstood simple expressions for decades. That I've been dead wrong.

Being an atheist means that no one but me has heard most of my best jokes. That they'll die with me. That any small acts of kindness were mostly to make myself feel better about myself and haven't made the world much better or counted toward any reward. Being an atheist means that writing is a mixed bag of solace, because, on the one hand, I can hope that someone can dig up one of my books in fifty years and find something they like but, on the other hand, I'll just be dead, dead, dead ("Death, death, death, death, death"). Cioran is the great poet of death.

> Life is nothing; death, everything. Yet there is nothing which is death, independent of life. It is precisely this absence of autonomous, distinct reality which makes death universal; it has no realm of its own, it is omnipresent, like everything which lacks identity, limit, and bearing: an indecent infinitude. (*The Trouble with Being Born*)

And in his furious belief in the overwhelming nothingness at the center of everything, he takes us out the other side to the small space where we live a little while; life is an aphorism—if we're lucky. Cioran is more amusing than many people think: "You are done for—a living dead man—not when you stop loving but stop hating. Hatred preserves: in it, in its chemistry, resides the 'mystery' of life." The spirit of Hazlitt lives.

For a long time, I admit, I hated the idea of belief in God or gods and even, I must admit, had great scorn and occasional pity for those who, as I saw it, indulged. I saw it as a great escapist cop-out from dealing with life, here and now, and the existential dilemma of death's finality. Now, my scorn has modified into perplexity. I could never mate with a believer, the way most Democrats could never settle down with a Republican. It's just a kind of cognitive dissonance: How can you vote for Jesus/Allah/Adonai, when Nothing is on the ticket? How can you think you might go somewhere when you die, when the alternative is eternal nothingness? When you can choose to embrace the horror of what death really is?

Death is a bland word. It should hiss and call for the speaker to recoil, the listener to back away. Cottage cheese, when it goes bad, should die. When we go, we should curdle.

> Priests and fools say
> We are but animate clay
> Just rude vessels
> Housing immortal souls
> But the dead only quickly decay
> They don't go about
> Being born and reborn
> And rising and falling like soufflé
> The dead only quickly decay
>
> STEPHIN MERRITT, "The Dead Only Quickly Decay"

Alternately, in the nineteenth century, John Brown's body lying "a-mouldering in the grave" has been attributed to William Steffe or to that greatest of all songwriters, anonymous, who tried to establish the parameters of the body's victory over the soul. When I was a boy, I was a bit puzzled and excited to sing a song about rotting in the grave. I wasn't sure what truth was marching on. Just that I was celebrating a body rotting in the grave. Truth was what really got buried. Hurray! "Mouldering" was a good vocabulary word. Sometimes we would sing, "John's brown body lies a-mouldering in the grave." Seemed a good bet. Then, "Gory, gory, hand it to ya."

Today's death: Ruth Greenglass. She fried the Rosenbergs. Perhaps the ghastliest part of the Rosenberg case was that so soon after the war, Jews in America were asked to burn other Jews. Hadn't there been enough of that? "Rue is for Ruth," from the book of Ruth. Years later, David Greenglass said he only testified that Ethel Rosenberg had typed up Commie spy notes because Ruth said she did. "I frankly think my wife did the typing, but I don't remember," this brother who sent his sister to die said. "So what am I going to do, call my wife a liar?" he said. So, get this, what David Greenglass is saying is that he had to choose to send his sister to die rather than call his wife a liar. Considering the kind of New York Jewish families I come from, this makes perfect sense. The whole case against Ethel Rosenberg revolves around typing. Who did the typing? Ruth worked as a typist for Louie Lefkowitz at the time, an assemblyman who went on to become a powerful attorney general. She was college bound, an honors student. But her mother made her take typing instead. She was typecast. So was Ethel. The prosecutors were Jewish: Irving Saypol and (good old) Roy Cohn. The judge was Jewish: Irving Kaufman. The defense attorneys were Jewish: Emanuel Bloch and Morton Sobell. When I think about the Rosenbergs, I think of the country creating a stage for postwar Jewish self-immolation. And creating the stereotype of the New York Commie Jew for a good two generations. I've always been fond of that stereotype.

When it came time to pick my mother's coffin, my father, brother, and I were all shell-shocked from months of cancer jack-in-the-box. Tumors had popped up everywhere, and denial had been the family's forced language, laid down like concrete by my father's will, with death only showing up sub rosa, the blades of grass of my brother's and my passing notice. When it came time to pick a box for the body that was lying in the bathroom, many thoughts fought for my attention. It was a little like buying a grief car. Spiffy model for the underground highway? Who was going to see it after the brief ceremony? Lead lined? Does the body decay more slowly? What does time matter anymore?

Do we look like cheapskates if we pick a simple wood coffin? Could we bear the thought of a quicker mouldering of what had so recently been a mother?

Apparently, since we chose one of the cheapest coffins offered to us—my memory tells me (this is almost thirty years ago) that our motive was respect. That a gaudy coffin wouldn't have suited my mother at all. As she was lowered into the ground in that plain box, the thought that occurred to me has not yet been altered: death makes life elementally grotesque, in an amusing kind of way. Cioran is one of the few writers able to completely capture this. "The fact that life has no meaning is a reason to live—moreover, the only one," he writes. But he means that life has no Meaning. Cioran's dark charm—and charm, not life, is the opposite of death, I think—is in this kind of bracing paradox. Life is, for the most part, a neutral, sometimes lifeless thing. For me, charm is the quintessence of wit brought to bear to amuse and delight another in our presence. It allows us to think, most briefly, that we exist with a kind of fluidly amusing grace that can be shared before we return to the stolidity of the solid motions of time and being. Charm makes us think we are invincible, perhaps even momentarily immortal. When Bergson wrote about the élan vital, he may have dreamt about one of the dances from *Swing Time* or *The Gay Divorcee*. That's one of the reasons Fred Astaire's death hit me so hard. The death of charm makes the ground tremble. At least, it made me tremble.

Nevertheless, as I write this, as I think of everything I've written so far in this essay, the horror of that final indignity—because that is what it continues to feel like to me—is inescapable. I've gone to visit my mother's grave on Long Island a few times since she died. It reminds me of the times I went with her to her parents' graves somewhere in Queens. She would pay these desultory old rabbis manqué to say kaddish over the graves. We would put the rocks on the headstones, markers that someone had been there, and go have some lunch. I would usually have a tuna fish sandwich.

But when I've visited my mother's grave, crying inconsolably as a man with a long lost mother, as a boy with a long lost mother, as a man who fears death because it will mean I can't read the *Times* and play with my son, can't digress, buy shoes, read a box score—I think denial is a very good thing sometimes. Maybe noble others, less neurotic, more philosophically balanced in their weltanschauungs, can live with the knowledge of their own deaths and the deaths of those they love more consistently. Or others just get deadened to death. Strike that metaphor. For me, death is still fresh out of the box. Or fresh in: Old Mother Death. I don't wake up and smell the roses. I wake up screaming.

Death is a motherfucker.

ON GIFTS

Proust, in *Guermantes Way*, writes, "Everything great that we know has come from neurotics . . . never will the world be aware of how much it owes to them, nor above all what they have suffered in order to bestow their gifts on it." That sentiment is a bit of gift-wish-fulfillment on for my part. If "the gift can circulate at every level of the ego," as Lewis Hyde says in his stunningly interesting *The Gift: Imagination and the Erotic Life of Property* (21), then mine might as well start with a little self-deprecation, since it is disappointment more than disgruntlement that has mostly driven my experience. I haven't gotten what I've wanted (you're looking at me with those "you're a member of a very large club" eyes), and I've frequently thought it wouldn't be that hard to give me what I wanted. The symbolism will be lost on no one. We can imagine our own pleasures and fail at delighting others, deciding instead to spend our time pouring our eyes over the dead carcass of delight in whatever form it takes. Our giving, focused on several weeks in December and the occasional birthday, is relegated to such bleak tidings. I must admit I long for more. Like Neil Young in "Heart of Gold," "I want to live, I want to give." (The two aren't mutually inclusive.) It's the anti-Garbo line. I don't vant to be alone.

I vant to give something that expressly suggests some small flash of sublimity, the excess of engagement. It may have worked for Garbo, but my face will not suffice.

~~~

My parents decided that my brother and I should receive presents for each other's birthday, with the caveat that the birthday boy would get a little more, a larger, more significant present, say, or two or three more presents. To use a cake metaphor, which seems apt, he'd get a larger slice. But this was culturally confusing, since my brother's birthday is December 25, the birthday beyond the pale of birthdays for Jewish children. I'm not sure if it felt that way to him. Perhaps, however, there was more than a method act in what I thought was the madness of his going to a yeshiva for a year, or part of a year, until he was terrified by the strangeness, the unfriendliness of what I and my other assimilated friends called "yammy-boppers" ("yammy" for *yarmulke*, or skull cap, wearers—even the word "yarmulke" is showing my age now, one of the Eastern European Yiddish words that younger Jews have been replacing with Israeli Hebrew words, in this case *kipah*, for the last twenty or thirty years). Perhaps my brother was giving the Jewish thing his all in the face of a name like Scott, and a birthday like Christmas, with presents suspiciously general to the season, even wrapped in silver sometimes, or perhaps, perish the thought, he believed the stuff, and my brother was actually a Jewish child exploring his belief and I wasn't and I'm playing out Freud's "family romance" as I always do, projecting backward.

Breathe. I digress. Nevertheless, our gift-giving rituals swirled around our Jewishness in different ways, some conventional, as in Chanukah, some bizarre and paradoxical, as in ersatz Christmas.

I developed a ritual for Christmas Eve and Christmas morning, with my mother's complicity, that I still lamely try to imitate, its aura distilled through a combination of giving and forbidding, since to even say Christmas in our house carried with it the slightly dizzy spell of transgression, as though one were cracking a door for an evil spirit, a *Christnik*. Despite this, after my grandparents died and I was liberated into my own room in the downstairs apartment of our row house, with a nine-inch black-and-white television all my own, my face three inches from the screen so that the characters looked like slightly larger insects, I began my own private ritual every Christmas Eve, watching Reginald Owen and Alastair Sim back-to-back in *A Christmas Carol* (1938) and *Scrooge* (1955), as some New York channel was in the habit of broadcasting every year. At some point while I was watching, between one and two o'clock, the door to the lower apartment would open, and I would hear footfalls on the carpeted stairs, my mother descending with our presents for the morning, gift central for the year, to place them in our playroom (another misnomer, it was a large dark storage room, formerly a living room—houses can be so Eastern European in their changeability). Yet it was not supposed to be a present bacchanal, hypothetically no larger than what we would receive for my birthday, but it was. It was, it was! A pile of presents for each of us, not two or three lovely presents, but a pile, a tower; and here comes the *fetish* that turns repeated memories into the impossible desire to repeat them, each pile was under a *towel*. They were towel-draped gift piles. Since my childhood, I have been longing for gifts under towels. Not particular towels. It's not like I'm longing for Egyptian cotton. Just the sight of the mysterious pyramid, the architectural gift offering.

The pyramid of gifts, domestically shrouded—but why a towel and not a sheet or blanket, since they were sleeping until the morning, a winter coat even, as though it were the stack that came in from the cold and my mother was the Santa figure (*nu* . . . ?) descending a staircase?

My mother stealthily crept upstairs. I would continue to watch my *Carol*, my *Scrooge*, coming out into the playroom during commercials to touch the pile (hold your letters—we've read the same books, all gone to therapy) and feel its magic carpet possibility. It was always the happiest time of the year for me, with these implicit gifts waiting to be opened, having been so softly delivered. I loved being alone with them, knowing they were meant for me. I would play a kind of charade with them, sort of getting a sense of their shapes, but not wanting to get too close to knowing, or guessing what was inside the packages, though occasionally I would have my desires confirmed, or possibly confirmed by the package size, some early-sixties spaceship set or pop gun, given away by the oblong box, a little coffin of a present.

I'd go back and forth between Alastair Sim—my favorite Scrooge of all time—and my gift pile. Even as an unrepentant Scrooge, he starts to melt fairly early on with a fierce sadness. Sim is an interesting actor, a scene stealer, though some feel annoyed by his tics, fine for the multiple roles of *The Bells of St. Trinians* but distracting elsewhere. But I love watching him in anything—his lively eyes could shift emotional gears so suddenly, their constant broadcasting of self-consciousness an interesting mirror for the viewer, who identifies with the actor in role who seems to be reading the world. As I do all my favorites: Bill Murray, Cary Grant, Judy Holliday, Edward Everett Horton, Fred Astaire . . . These performances always seem like gifts to me, like little missives that were sent just to me, always somehow freshly timed: Horton's double takes, or the way Judy Holliday starts to walk and stops to think, or Fred Astaire in any kind of motion, Cary Grant asking a question, the way his voice starts to rise with a slightly perceptible smile . . .

When the two Scrooges ended, I had the difficult job of going to sleep with the gift-towel tactility quivering in my mind. It was all I could do to get two or three hours before spring up at dawn, the permissible hour of present opening, rousing my brother for our Roman free-for-all, the towel pulled asunder like the invitation to a bacchanal. The rest was paper flying, murmurs of orgasmic delight or disappointment: "Thank your mother," my father would always say. "She did the work." He was discounting his own rhetoric as slaving to make money for the family, a rhetoric of work, which produced the money that enabled my mother's labor to purchase the gifts. A complicated and transparent gambit that we appreciated and saw through.

I do remember clearly my mother's face as she recorded my reactions to all the presents, now that I focus on the narrative denouement; gratitude is the middle stage of gift giving according to Hyde (between giving and reciprocation). Her face was bemused and delighted by my analysis of what was wonderful, what good, and what, well, perhaps, slightly off the mark. How frighteningly close to my adult self, without, you know, the delightful self-consciousness. The generosity in her tolerance of my puckishness was lovely, and I've felt a mournful and bittersweet sense of pending disappointment every Christmas Eve since her death.

It's a bit of a silly question, of course unanswerable, literally, since my mother is dead, and because it was probably just a moment's passing fancy: what about that towel was supposed to keep the mystery until morning? It did and it didn't, though towels have never been the same. Death robs us of the answers to simple questions. We forget that one of our lives' simple gifts is the answer to a question.

Gifts were a constant ritual at our house. My father, a travel agent, in exchange for a favor here and there, had almost free rein to pick up samples at many Garment District businesses. This meant that, two or three times a week sometimes, he would arrive home with oblong cardboard boxes filled with three, four, five dresses or outfits for my mother, gifts ostensibly for her. My mother would serve my father dinner (he ate alone—it would be seven o'clock or so by the time he got home). And then my mother would, while my father ate, perform her fashion show. He ate. She dressed and undressed. *I know.* And I know you know. But they didn't know. And I didn't know then. Oh, let's get it out in the open: the shiver of the men's club. Not that my mother was coming out belting her version of "Hey, Big Spender!" But structurally. Thinking about it now, the combination of dining and display . . . Was my father bringing himself a present, or my mother? Well, both, of course. And the casual frisson of the pornographic? Well, at the very least, we'll just leave that to my astute younger self.

Occasionally, I wonder if my mother tired of running back and forth, dressing and undressing at the end of the day. (Counterargument: please, David, can't you reconstruct a more innocent, less complicated, more purely benign narrative? Clothes were brought home. Your mother tried them on. She was happy with new clothes. Here, a Bugs Bunny voice intrudes: *Uh, maybe, Doc. But I don't think so.*) They evaluated the outfits. The good, the bad, the indifferent. Ninety percent of them were lodged in cheap metal clothes chests in our garage, which started resembling a metastasized Lower East Side secondhand shop. I remember my mother saying, "More?" and my father saying, "That's all right, honey. There's more where that came from."

My father would also promise to bring things home for me sometimes, frequently things he could get from his many clients, who worked in not only the garment business but all kinds of businesses, including Alexander's Department Stores, once a storied name in New York retail. These gifts were usually announced with, "I can get it for you," as though "wholesale" were just an utterance away, even when I was quite young. My father would promise these in response to some vague desire of mine or occasionally to some plan to buy something that he could get from a client gratis. I was always thrilled when he first annunciated this, even after years of disappointment (children are so selectively gullible). And then began the waiting game and my metaphorical ulcers (read: anxiety). I would ask my mother when she was talking to my father on the phone if he had gotten "it," the object of desire, the requested gift. I would wait at the door for my father to come home to see if "it" had come with him. "Tomorrow," he would say definitively.

What are the compunctions of timeliness for gift giving? I know there are cultural rules about wedding gifts not going past the one year mark, from watching a recent episode of *Curb Your Enthusiasm*, my guide to all laws *ad absurdum*. But what about generally? By when does a gift have to be delivered? When do you have to put up? When does a late birthday gift seem like an early Christmas present? I became so desperate for whatever it was I wanted I could no longer think about anything else. "Tomorrow" became never. I thought my father was dodging my phone calls at work. Think about it—my own father was avoiding my calls! It turned me, over the years, into Mr. Immediate Gratification, as in if you show me the present, you give me the present. I have trouble delaying purchase of anything, delaying anything as a matter of fact. It's most inconvenient.

Eventually, I imagine, I must have been gifted or denied. I must have been exhausted or satisfied. But not after a promise of a gift had been stretched to the breaking point or beyond. That's why I prefer to never announce a gift or, when I do announce it, to make it my business to deliver, as though I were a bloodhound on the trail of a gift with four legs.

~~~

What do I want?

Clothes, beautiful clothes! But like Joseph, the one coat or shirt that, magically, outdoes all others. It might be a black shirt. Despite all my black clothes, I've mined for years for the perfect black shirt. It's the fit, slightly loose but not formless; the fabric, probably a blend (linen is too stiff, cotton doesn't have the hang, silk would be too . . . silky); and what of the buttons: shiny black or silvery shapes? My ex-wife was the only person to shop this for me. Usually, women are afraid to buy me clothes. Oh, how can too many be perfect?

Responses to gifts, both internally and expressively, are central to what delights and vexes us about giving gifts. We're told, when young, to look delighted when Aunt Sarah gives us our gift at the party this afternoon. What pressure, and what confusingly sophisticated and potentially hypocritical advice that can be. Don't give your true feelings away. And convincingly act out the opposite of how you feel. Of course, we're trying to teach children gratitude, how to not hurt feelings. But couldn't we spare them and merely teach politeness without instructing delight in advance? "Remember to say thank you, no matter what the present is." How I dislike the false gushing over trivial, inappropriate, and downright grotesque presents that are the bastard children of these childhood injunctions.

Especially when so many people spend so little time in their selection of presents. I can see mustering up some luster that isn't completely authentic when I've been presented with a present whose symbolic value seems great to the giver or when the giver has missed the mark despite clearly trying to individualize the present, to hit the mark of me, delight me, find the gift that seems to know me. This giver deserves a performance, a bow, some fealty from his brother in giftery, or her lover, whatever the case may be. "I love it," "That's so me"—I'll give them enough schmaltz to last the season.

I feel especially sensitive to this when I think about the times when my performance was subpar, when I didn't give the gift of guttural responsiveness about the gift that gave me less than what I thought I wanted, and clearly disappointed the giver. A recipe for guilt. I'll tell you one that speaks terribly of me in retrospect, even in context.

I have an aversion to kitsch, unless it's historical kitsch that I find interesting or amusing in a particular way: World's Fair stuff, old cartoon lunch boxes, fine. Don't ever give me anything with puppies, kittens, flags, hearts, etc. Please. About thirty years ago, teetering unhappily in a relationship that was to go on doing so for some years, my once and future girlfriend gave me a tin carousel music box for Christmas. It was about fourteen inches high and eight inches wide—rather large. And the horses, copper-colored tin, sat flimsily and lopsidedly on their poles. There was a copper-colored tin flag on top that snapped off the first time I tried to straighten it. A big thing for what it was. And when you wound the key, it played that depression standby (we were constantly on depression standby), "Happy Days Are Here Again." She wanted me to be touched. I thought she was touched, giving me what looked like a trinket on steroids. I wanted something that *spoke to me*. But, of course, she wanted me to speak to her. Like the Grinch, my gift heart was too small. "Thanks, really." I wasn't rude. I was pinched, not entirely convincing. But, of course, it was an entirely sentimental gift that deserved an openhearted response. I can try to justify myself (isn't that a bore?) with the details of the relationship, but age teaches us the severe pleasures of merely saying how wrong we were, how wrong I was, how sad. How pinched. This, of course, is the gift of hard won knowledge, sometimes difficult to accept and say thank you for. It really was a lovely present.

There have been other occasions where my reaction has been less than enthralled and where I think my culpa is more complicated. Some friends one has gift relationships with; and other friends not. And it can be tricky measuring the vectors of friendship on this scale alone, although one does *tend*, I think, to exchange gifts with the friends one is closest to. There are exceptions, of course. Some people just do not *do* gifts. If you gift them, they will accept awkwardly and not reciprocate, breaking what Lewis Hyde calls the circle of gift giving. They might act strangely, as though they couldn't imagine why you would be giving them a present on December 25 or on their birthday. They haven't, let's say, the gift-giving temperament. Or they grew up in a particularly bleak house or dour orphanage. Perhaps their Scrooge of a father never got a visit from Jacob Marley—he got hit by a ghost truck.

Gratitude is so tricky. It, too, is worthy of an essay of its own. Where does the line between gratitude and response efface? I want to delight someone, but I don't want them to feel as though they owe me something. But is that completely honest? I want them to feel that I've loved and cared. Yet when I gift, can I ever say there isn't an ulterior motive? Am I ever not trying to buy a bit of love, even if it's with love?

Other friends and lovers, husbands, wives, relatives, at times, seem not to return the care you give to the presents you choose for them. Not all gifts are equally individuated: special, inspired, blundered upon . . . it would be a second job to be fully creative with all gifts. Some gifts are cupid gifts, an arrow shot from your knowledge of the person to the idea or thing you happen to think of. Pure kismet. Others are merely excellent choices, showing you know your recipient, an offering based on understanding, on listening and attention. Still others, small symbolic offerings to an idea or a strong sense of practical need. When my reaction has been less than excited, the forced smile, a bit automatic, no matter how hard I've tried to appear really pleased, it's mostly because I've felt I've been given *anygift*, something that could have been given to anyone, the generic thing that was taken out of the gift box in the closet when a gift was required.

It seems to me that one can avoid that trap with even a little bit of foresight and attention. When those close to me have given me mediocre books culled from the season's lists (*A Natural History of the Fountain Pen*, a pox on anyone who uses "A Natural History of" ever again in a title) or music that seems to combine the popular flavors of the week (*An Introduction to Cuban-Malian Klezmer String Pickers!*), I know that they're moving fast to discharge a gift obligation, and my genial politesse expresses itself while I'm thinking, "Couldn't you have shown that you know something specific about me?" I must admit I could feel worse about these reactions, even if they smell a bit of the ingrate. (The rub: you should feel grateful that anyone is buying you presents at all!)

But wait—should I feel grateful that anyone is buying me presents at all? In the grand scheme of a cruel, terrible, brutal, finite, miserable world, sure. I mean, as my parents might have said, "It beats a punch in the nose." Or a slap in the face. Although, a really bad gift can feel like an affront. Like a slap in the face. "No, no, no," you're saying, "hypersensitive boy, at least the impulse to give is being preserved; you're still being gifted, being given something." But I fear the automatic pilot of actions, like those computer programs where you can combine what you automate what you usually do and have the computer fulfill the process with a stroke. I want to have a sense of process with my gifts.

"You're impossible to buy gifts for." This is a refrain I've heard many times in my life. Admittedly, I do have a reasonable quantity of stuff in my life, notably music and books. And I do have rather specific tastes. But join the club. Ironically, though, the people who say this usually buy me excellent gifts, although sometimes it takes some prodding: "Oh, not really!"

What too many CDs or books has meant is, clearly, pretty subjective. One person's cache is another person's overflow, stacks everywhere as a kind of long-term home decorating strategy or a reason to call in support services. But it seems to me that anyone who has "too many" of something is reasonably easy to buy presents for if you're a person with some imagination. After all, you only have to buy them one book by the thousands of writers or one CD (or MP3) by the thousands of composers or singers that they don't already have! They have all of Leonard Bernstein's Mahler? Great—buy them Bruno Walter or Georg Solti. They have the Donald Frame Montaigne? Get them the Screech or the Ives. You have many more informed choices to make than with the person whose library is skimpy, whose musical taste is tepid. People with eclectic tastes tend to love having the gaps in their collections filled. Even if she hasn't been actively craving it, the odds are she's anal enough to want it in her musical or literary library. Or be even more esoteric and daring. Do they have Bach's *Preludes and Fugues*? Buy them Shostakovich's *Preludes and Fugues*. Music and books are not the only gifts in the world, of course. Movies, jewelry, clothes!

My own tastes have been asserting themselves, clearly (possibly as primers to those who have or might give); but antiques, collections of buttons, art supplies, cigars, James Bond regalia, Nabokovian butterfly collections . . . everyone has her or his vector of interest, and if it veers to the mundane, it is our role as gift giver (I was about to say "job," but I'm resisting the vocabulary of work—as opposed to labor—a distinction nicely made by Lewis Hyde, which carries with it the air of drudgery) to either give them the mundane stuff they love or take a leap of faith and try to startle them with something new. Why, by the by, do you have friends who are so boring!

I don't mean to (people always mean to, at least a little, when they start with "I don't mean to," a companion to "pun unintended") sound condescending, but I think many people want present buying to be easy. Sometimes, life is busy and we don't particularly want to do it. So we look for reasons for not doing it terribly well. "You're impossible to buy presents for!"

What do I want?

What's my fantasy gift?

Have I ever come close to being satisfied? That may be begging the question. Fulfillment is such a tricky thing. Does admitting it call down the gods, or denying it? Call me insatiable (call me irresponsible), a giftaholic who is constructing an elaborate edifice around his neurotic needs (call me unreliable . . . not so good, I realize, for an essayist) or perhaps a neurotic with impossible standards? I didn't answer the question, did I? I'll say this: My son made me a writing box, with black-and-white checkerboard design, a little notebook inside, and a pen. I've never had a better present.

~~~

I simply had to buy ex libris stamps for my mother. What felt at first like a good idea developed into an urge, an obsession, tinged with some sense that mysterious forces were conspiring against me in this gift quest. I didn't know then that, as is so often the case, the force at work was time. Buying a gift can take on the quality of a quest. You feel as though this were the only gift in Christendom (an entirely inappropriate word in my case) that were the proper match for the receiver, that no one, in fact, had ever dreamed such a perfect pairing, the Fred and Ginger of gift and gifted, meant to open to each other, move about the room together. Have you ever felt that compulsion, that need to give that single thing that was meant for someone that you knew you had to procure, buy, arrange . . . no matter what? I mean, I'm not talking about having the circus on their lawn here. I grew up in Gravesend, in Brooklyn. I don't buy people houses or cars, or trips to Europe or Harry Winston baubles. But excluding the effulgence's of the rich, there is a world of perfect presents with the names of your brothers, lovers, mothers, children, and friends on them. In any case, the bookplate idea hit me in my last year of college in a small town in Vermont. My mother loved to read and had collected a small library's worth of popular literature and English history, which she had scattered in piles about the back room of our row house, which we merrily called the "den" (as opposed to "small back room with bars on the little window and Naugahyde love seat and oversized TV and big piles of books with a door that led to the fire escape").

I believe I had seen an ex libris stamp on library books, and the William Morris–inspired designs along with the thought of her Anglophilia, all of her books, the years of watching her sit at our small Formica dining room table with a slice of buttered challah and large jar of Breakstone's cottage cheese as her coffee cup, book propped on a metal book holder, probably sealed the gift idea. I went to the local bookstore, severely limited in books but with that kind of toney bookstore feel, cards and gifts on walnut shelves and a matronly cashier with classes that hung around her neck. I registered her as smart in that class-accented and alert way one gets used to in New England, but she looked at me as though I were stupid when I asked her if there was any way I could order ex libris stamps and have them engraved. I wasn't trying to be . . . anything. I called them that because I didn't have the word "bookplate"; "ex libris" had been on the stamp. We did a kind of classic Abbott and Costello routine, my pronouncing it, her trying it after me, saying things like "a wheat press," until I wrote it down and then explained what I meant. This was in 1978, so catalogs were the thing, and she actually managed to dig up an old catalog that I could order "let's just call them bookplates, young man" from. I placed the order, but something always seemed to go wrong in actually getting them.

My mother's birthday passed. Months passed. I went to graduate school in California. When I was in bookstores, I would tell myself that I had to renew my quest, that the perfect gift still had to be bought somehow, and I would experience a wave of anxiety knowing that I had made this discovery, which would give my mother so much pleasure, but wasn't coming any closer to materializing it. And I realize in the telling of this anecdote the number of markers of class in the story, which were undoubtedly part of the reason for my anticipated pleasure: those little . . . bookplates were tiny doormats to another class for me, a different cultural class, achieved through books, which my parents, and especially mother, had given me. I was attempting, without knowing it at the time, to give my mother both pleasure and a symbolic acknowledgment of this.

On a return visit from California, there was actually an old phone message from the bookshop asking if I still wanted the stamps. And here, time goes into dizzying acceleration, because my mother was moments from her fatal diagnosis of lung cancer. The gift that got away, those ex libris stamps would have been marvelous, but I never got to getting them. And I reminded myself that even though my getting away to graduate school in California was also a gift, I had finished my work and decided immediately to move back east to help take care of her. This did not feel like my gift to her, but instead like a roiling combination of necessity, love, and obligation. I am still too stern with myself to see it as a gift, alas. But when I distance myself from my younger self, I can see it as a gift of sorts. Perhaps she knew better, having been so generous with her children.

There should be a word, "longing to give," a German word? Something like *unheimlich*?

~~~

Names are gifts, full of Charisma: bestower of gifts by the Holy Spirit. Names can be gifts, and I haven't named my mother, the litany of "my mothers": Rhoda—derived from Rose (her mother). It can also mean, "from Rhodes" (originally named for its roses). Backward, it sounds like *adore*.

~~~

What do I want?
A full-sized antique carousel, in a building attached to my house that holds it alone. I dreamed that I had it one time, with some

other rides that were broken, and some that worked, and no one was around. My own abandoned night carnival. It thrilled me.

The Freudian implications of childhood wish fulfillment, since the carousel is a huge toy, pumped up with the sexual undercurrent of a child's experience of a carousel ride. No wonder I couldn't respond to my girlfriend's gift: too innocently loaded.

Then I dreamed a few years ago that I was alone in a basement wonderland of carousels, with horses gashed by their poles and left to die, some moving perfectly . . . labyrinthine, mirrored. What should have been scary was spookily soothing, as though Luna Park in Coney Island was slowly resurrecting and healing my neurasthenic self.

~~~

Giving oneself gifts has an excellent rationale behind it. It takes some of the edge off wanting others to respond too much in kind to your gifts, no matter how naturally the circle of gift exchange might be. When I buy myself gifts, I frequently veer into the realm of collecting: posters, vintage clothes, books, books, books. Since a full discussion of collecting may digress me unground, I should confine myself to those times when one buys oneself something special. When an occasion is being marked, either as what Lewis Hyde calls a "threshold" or an accomplishment, or when a gift is in some other way necessary. I was trained early on in an economy of punishment and reward, and the reward has been as insistent in the ways I've conducted my peculiar life as the punishments have been. Not all rewards are gifts, of course. The expensive mousse cakes that I kept buying myself to get through my comprehensive exams, breaking every twenty minutes for a forkful during sixteen-hour days of study, were

Pavlovian wheel turners, carrots (but what indulgently delightful carrots they were!), as opposed to real gifts, things I gave myself, things that were bestowed, that had some symbolic, as opposed to practical, value.

A gift for the self that marks an accomplishment (in my case, publishing a book or having gotten tenure or a promotion) usually comes with the idea that you somehow deserve this. The gift is the whipped cream. It self-confirms the worth that has been symbolically awarded. The world likes your work! Your audience liked your words. So you can like you. Here's a first edition to mark the occasion and really confirm that something good has happened, now certified by the David market. The neurotic problem attending this is that I experience, frequently, a frisson of buyer's guilt after the purchase. In other words, the gift curdles, or the reason for buying it does. I feel as though I had done something self-indulgent, unnecessary, that I had merely looked for an excuse for buying myself something. And I chase the confirmation back up the great chain of validation. However, that doesn't seem to stop me the next time. Moses supposes neurosis.

Another version of the present to me from me is based on how simply miserable I'm feeling and/or how terrible some experience has been, actually or melodramatically. This is the self-pity pick-me-up or materialist self-soother. It shows I want to take care of myself and I'm not quite sure how, so I try to turn into my mother. I buy myself a toy and see if I feel better. See that gabardine jacket from the fifties? This has been a really hard time for me. I'm going to buy it for me. OK, honey? Yes. Thanks.

But does it really work as a token of esteem, a change in the course of the river of bad runs? Or is it merely an excuse for that conspicuous commodity you couldn't otherwise justify?

There have been times when I've wondered if I weren't feeling worse than I should so I could justify buying myself a gift to feel better. When the trouble is deep, the water wide, someone ill, the self-gift can seem like the most narcissistically disposable of purchases, no matter how golden its prospects once were.

Celebration is the core of gift giving, even its most sober variety. And one of the essential qualities of the gift is its ripple, its afterlife. The afterlife of a compensatory gift may be all too brief, its onanistic impetus becoming uncomfortably clear.

~~~

What do I want?
All I want for Christmas is my two front teeth.
All I want is a room somewhere.
All I really, really want our love to do
Is to bring out the best in me and you (Joni Mitchell)

The last requires the gift of hard work, perhaps votives.

~~~

What do I want?

The symphony I've never heard that takes me on a journey to perfect peace. I don't know this composer, though apparently she knows me; and when I hear the last notes of the last movement, a minor miracle occurs and I'm gifted with a lifting of anxiety and a sense of my own harmonic possibilities.

~~~

When does friendship take on the quality of a gift—when does it feel like one? Not that it lacks reciprocity, but that it is so generously given. Two friends come immediately to mind: my friends Lois and Steve. Lois has been the closer friend. We met when she was a professor and I was a graduate student working on my PhD, and I served as her assistant at our school's London program for a year. We seemed to pass over the student/teacher thing and go right into friendship, and for that year and in the years I had left in my program, I became something of a family appendage, in all the best senses. Our friendship began twenty-nine years ago—if my clock had eyes, they'd have just widened a bit—and in those years, my friends have never missed a chance to do whatever they could for me in any way. Lois and I have our long chats about the state of our worlds, grounding talks. Steve (a law professor and former dean at the same university) and Lois have invited me and then me and my son on vacations to Texas and Mexico, their home away from home. Steve always attends to my son joyously, in the pool, on his kayak . . . Lois has always bolstered me in bleak times, when I've been stupid or beyond melancholy. In a maladroit stage of exiting a relationship. Puzzling the expressionistic halls of academe. If I ever needed anything, their door would be open. They were my second family when my first had dissipated. They flew from Houston to Columbus for my wedding; for other friends, this was an inconvenience. When I was working on my PhD, Lois guided me through minefields with encouragement and advice, suggesting I neither give up nor make an idiot out of myself (never in those terms).

This kind of friendship—where *what can we do for you?* is virtually automatic—is beyond the bounds of excellent friendship. It is one of the clearest gifts I've had. But on top of that has been emotional honesty, not just acceptance. In my epic lunches with Lois, we talk about almost everything. To gild the lily, they have given me one of my most precious gifts: a large coy, ceramic *muerta* (a Mexican Day of the Dead figure, in skeleton form). She's about eighteen inches tall, her lithe boney hand cradling the side of her head. She's in wedding garb—a brown skirt and brown beret-like wedding cap. I've had her—or she, me—for many years now. She can see right through me. Just what I need.

~~~

Rousseau, in Lausanne, was in tough shape. He was a kid, bouncing around, pining for Mamma, Mme. de Warens. He lodged with an innkeeper, knowing he couldn't pay, and in the morning, offered his coat as recompense. In *The Confessions*, he writes, "The good fellow refused, saying that, Heaven be praised, he had never stripped anyone. . . . I was touched by his kindness, but less touched than I should have been, and less so than I have been since when I have thought of this incident again." Rousseau tells us that this simple gift was more "worthy of gratitude" than "services no doubt more important, but rendered with greater ostentation." An alternate meaning, perhaps, for simple gifts.

~~~

Lewis Hyde writes, "It is because gift exchange is an erotic form that so many gifts must be refused" (72–73). Refused or avoided. Perhaps this is crucial. We're not comfortable with the creative intimacy, the erotic nature, of asserting our attachments to others, the ways we do and might know each other, especially in our culture, where there is a whiff of homophobia attached to attachment that manifests too openly. Still too true among men, at least, who don't, in my experience, buy each other presents often. We understand clear-cut erotic refusals. But I think this fear turns the pleasure principle of gift giving, the delights of its labor, into work. The vitality of gift exchange is refused, I think, out of fear. Perhaps one needs to be a little emotionally bisexual to love buying gifts and not fear the sources of one's inspiration. Let's have gift therapy!! New schools, new programs: doctorates in giftology. I've clearly watched *The Wizard of Oz* too many times. There, at the end, those wonderful creatures get powerful gifts.

~~~

Some other wonderful gifts I've received—what do they say about me, my subject? A handmade set of small circular cardboard boxes from my ex-wife, each covered, alternately, with photos of our son, her, and me. The one covered with photos of me is particularly striking—how could it not be? Me at all angles, at all ages, glaring, sneering, warm, and containing paper clips, so that a shifting kaleidoscope of my visages is in my hands several times a day. Another gift, sent by my father, when I bought my first house: an antique Spanish console table and Spanish side table, a large beveled mirror that had belonged to my maternal grandparents, two large cubist paintings, painted by a distant relative, all of which I had growing up. In addition, two chests made of dark cherry, the contents of whose drawers I had carefully examined as a kid, out of intense curiosity, Oedipal and otherwise. My son will no doubt do the same, see what he finds in back of his parents' drawers to shock and amuse him at eight or fourteen. Some years ago, a good friend who had always claimed I'm impossible to buy for simply zinged me at Christmas with this: a Belgian miniposter of *A Matter of Life and Death* and a small Spanish poster of *The Apartment*, both in mint condition! Two of my pantheon films, directed respectively by Michael Powell and Billy Wilder! This was a one-two punch that showed how well he knew me, and the pleasure of my knowing his knowing that was as great as the gifts themselves. All these gifts had a view: toward the past; all were gifts with dimension, depth, history.

~~~

What do I want?

Ask the Sibyl of Cumae or Tithonus.

~~~

What do I want?

A celestial emissary bearing a signed letter guaranteeing I'll live until my son is thirty.

~~~

What do I want to give?

The gift whose delight is like honey from the Psalms, a gift that maketh the receiver so grateful that they love me to death.

~~~

Is health, longevity, a gift, if we take away those smart things we do for ourselves, such as exercising and eating well? We think of luck as a gift sometimes, a gift of genetics or accident; a bus hasn't hit us, and those diagnoses stayed benign. The combinations of circumstances worked to our advantage. The Yiddish word *mechiah* has something of that flavor but more of the moment, with an additive of pleasure. You're sitting outside in a chair, and a nice breeze comes your way, the air perfectly matching your skin temperature. "It's a mechiah," you say, a gift, not directly from God or anyone or anything else. It's almost Eastern in its flavor. You've just been given something, perhaps by some pantheistic ally; it's sourceless, but it feels like an offering. You accept it.

What about that Great American Gift: $ (not *just* American certainly, but can any other compare?). Certainly it's the gift *par excellence* from parent to child (my father has never, I think, given me a birthday present that wasn't money) and even occasionally, depending on the domestic arrangement, from a spouse too. Well, the fact is that money can be a liberating gift to children at the right time, offering them opportunities that they long for, that they need in order to stay ahead of the separation curve. But it's also classically gendered. Women buy presents; fathers give cash. Ugh. "I don't know what to get them," they say, and I've seen a few scratching their heads like Dagwood Bumstead. Most unattractive. So they reach for those Hallmark cards with the handy inserts and stick a couple of twenties in. Cowards of capital. (And here again, the old voice . . . *better than a slap in the face.*)

~~~

In any discussion of gifts, one wants to be careful of the possibility *épater le bourgeois.* The thingness of presents can overwhelm, sugarplums, whether from Amazon—the one you really want, the 21,332nd best-selling item, as opposed to the 445,556th *thing,* which is what you got (*Damn, the aura leaked!*)—or Etsy, or the crafty hands of your beloved. But let's concede the point that we are living in a material world and can extrapolate from there. Emerson, in his essay "Gifts," takes a radical stand against the bought gift:

> Rings and other jewels are not gifts, but apologies for gifts. The only gift is a portion of thyself. Thou must bleed for me. Therefore the poet brings his poem; the shepherd, his lamb; the farmer, his corn; the miner, a gem; a sailor, coral and shells; the painter, his picture; the girl, a handkerchief of her own sewing. . . . But it is a cold, lifeless business when you go to the shops to buy me something.

Well, Emerson, I'm with you in spirit, sort of. The lawyer, her briefs; the programmer, her program; the psychic, his future; the housewife . . . her children? Plenty of blood in those I suppose. The girl, her handkerchief? It's such a gendered romantic image that it made me want to cry and choke. I think Emerson, metrosexual *avant la lettre*, is really thinking of what he wants from Thoreau, though how he's going to get shells and gems . . . no, no, of course, the best present of all: an essay, right?

And as for jewels not being gifts: Kobe Bryant.

I think diamonds are beautiful, in the way that I think kaleidoscopes are beautiful, or prisms, sun catchers. They've all become part of the American iconic kitsch establishment. It's absolutely impossible to look at a diamond flawlessly, bound up as they are with the Stone Age of marriage mythology. I have some sentiment left for my parents' generation—late 1940s, early 1950s—who saved for their karat or so, if they were lucky enough to hit the postwar gravy train. And am I being sexist if I, even while rolling my retrospected eyes, understand that Richard Burton, born into miserable poverty in Wales, having survived the RAF in WWII, may have actually thought he needed to have something gaudy and expensive in his pocket to give to Liz. But Liz, Liz, Liz stoked the gaudy, glittery, bauble gift factory for forty years demanding karats and karats and karats . . . as though Bugs Bunny could never get a fix. And all the while, she showed that, paradoxically, diamonds are not a girl's best friend, unless you mean that they're mostly better friends than her choice of husbands.

Diamonds are supposedly "classy," sold with a hushed male voice on TV commercials telling us what *she* really wants and needs, as though *he* were *her* subconscious. Diamonds are clearly scary. Run away from diamonds! In one commercial, a yuppieish guy screams, "I love you," in an anonymous Italian piazza. In front of a church! (*Who do you love?*) Pigeons scatter! She covers his mouth. He gives her a diamond ring instead. The message is clear. Don't be too crazy when you're in love; spend too much money on an insanely expensive present that the culture tells you Liz Taylor craved. And ironically, she was the most astonishing natural beauty. Gradually weighed down by all that adornment.

In Emersonian terms, Kobe Bryant's ring gift—a $4 million, eight-karat purple diamond—is the purest apology for a gift one could imagine. It shocks and awes beyond what you might think your level of even Hollywood-style vulgarity could achieve. It wasn't a weapon of a present, an attempt to beat the offended into submission. I keep seeing twenty huge Tudor houses lined up with an equal sign next to them and a small box next to the equal sign. But make no mistake: the message was, "I have bought a huge diamond apology for a permanent pass."

Mere excess never creates a successful gift. Nor when the gift is given under duress, such as a gift-cum-ransom.

Here's an idea. Let's have a moratorium on expensive love gems, de rigueur for the wedding set, until men are sport solitaires. Until diamonds are a boy's best friend, this is one gift I think we've seen enough of—it's done enough damage, economic and cultural (no engagement ring for the man, remember). When the voiceover, a woman, says, "She knows what he truly wants," let's talk again.

~~~

I haven't said much about what I've given, and I think there are a couple of good reasons for that. The most obvious is no one should crow about what a good job she or he has done. I was taught better. Certainly, I might say a thing or two about how giving a certain gift made me feel. Though secondary, of course, to how the gift was received. And to this, one can't speak with any certainty except from the proverbial gift horse's mouth. It would be presumptuous to say someone loved a gift, even if one were pretty certain (my father, not having seen for thirty years or so the photograph of his nuclear family when he was ten or so that I had restored, enlarged, and framed for his seventy-fifth birthday, seemed visibly moved—but maybe he would rather have not been taken back that far, that day; maybe my own sentimentality served itself more than him). Because the heart of a recipient is always a little dark. And this is the leap of faith a giver commits to, always hoping but never knowing if a gift is serving the receiver more than the giver. The old joke about the kid giving his father a baseball cap extends to a generalized theory of gift giving as narcissistic. Giving what we want, giving what we want the other to want, which is us, always us. As Lewis Hyde says, "gifts are the agents of a spirit that survives the consumption of its individual embodiments" (48). As we give, so shall we want to please, and so shall we want to embody ourselves in both the gift and, if we're not careful, the recipient. So I won't speak to my success as giver, but I will tell you that for better or worse I pay attention. For my brother's fiftieth birthday, I spent months accumulating stuff from our childhood: photographs, obscure store items, regalia, music—and sent him a memory box he seemed to like. I bought an ex-girlfriend a first edition of Millay with her favorite adolescent poem. She liked that, too.

I know you'll have objections to this or that, to what I've said. Giving gifts is sensitive, personal, potentially painful. But if you've stayed with me this long, I've been gifted by your attention.

Why should we give at all? Perhaps Emerson is right, that we should just love. That gifts are trivial in love's shade. Martial says that "gifts are hooks," an unpleasant idea, which binds the recipient to the giver through gratitude, as though gratitude were an insinuating kind of emotional slavery. "You shouldn't have," we hear people say all the time; and in that, is there is an implicit, "Now I must"? Or to change tenses, "If you hadn't, I wouldn't now have to." The incommensurate sense of gift giving can defeat the idea of giving the specific gift. Walter Benjamin says in "One Way Street" that "gifts must affect the receiver to the point of shock," which is the camp I've always been in, more or less, and a sentiment not as inconsistent as it first seems with Emerson (the flowing gift is an overflowing gift) though also not as antagonistic to the purchase (a rare book for Benjamin?). But, of course, we can't *always* give that stirringly, that Cupid gift. Nevertheless, giving is an instinct, I think, a celebratory instinct born of our desire to share and celebrate, which should be refined into an artful and knowledgeable enterprise. Without our ability to give, we would be less interesting, a grayer form of laboring creature, unrewarded, less remarked. The forms of labor that we institutionalize to celebrate our specific selves are potentially very good things. If we can skip over certain narcissistic traps (giving what we want and what we want the receiver to want) and learn to enjoy the process of listening and finding, gifting can be one of the best things we do. Design a very strange day for your lover, complete with stops with views, small gifts with moving parts, and photographs she didn't know you had. Give your friend his favorite childhood food. How did he know you knew them? Watch your kid's favorite's movies all day long. That's such a simple one, but act out any part she wants.

~~~

What do I want?
It's under a towel—did you guess this already?

Only one present this year.

I'll watch Alistair Sim and Reginald Owen, in reverse order, beginning with repentance, and ending with the cold inertia of the Scrooge heart.

Everything slows, footsteps down, she drapes a towel over her head.

I pull slowly, and pause—the wrong time might stop the heart.

I promise, I promise, I won't look until dawn.

SELF-PORTRAIT

FRANCIS BACON'S DEFORMITY

I cannot watch myself fall asleep. I will not see myself die. And even with double mirrors, I will never see myself as an unreflected living image, never have the image of my face in three dimensions; it is the one visible object in the world that I can never see. This built-in distortion of self-image can be, in what may strike you as an about-face, a useful denial, if you see what I mean. And then, perhaps, when I notice the distortion in others, because of a sense of my own grotesqueness, the grotesqueness of others is muted.

I offer this as a preliminary theory of Francis Bacon's self-portraits' relationship to the rest of his work, the writhing bodies that seem to have escaped from Bosch only to end up locked up in some profoundly anonymous and claustrophobic room sometime in the twentieth century.

Plastically and organically, the face is always in motion. We can never dive into the Heraclitian river with the same face twice. We have never freed ourselves from reactions of terror when we perceive the nature of our natures explicit in physiognomy. Part of the horror of any physical representation is the decay implicit in the life of living matter, and even though at every moment we are undergoing a kind of epidermal and cellular meltdown (the idea of which forces us to see the skeletons under skin), the relatively slow pace of decay encourages us to see, paradoxically, that individually we are small variations on a theme of complex carnality—slightly more so than our bestial kin—and on each other. We are statically dissolving. Thus, perhaps, the inescapable fluidity and figuratively graphic animality of Bacon's human figures. Static pools suggesting definite shapes in the process of evaporating. This essentially profane vision of human nature is amoral and spiritually bleak: why Francis Bacon discomforts.

~~~

The secret is too plain. The pity of it smarts,
Makes hot tears spurt: that the soul is not a soul,
Has no secret, is small, and it fits
Its hollow perfectly: its room, our moment of attention.
That is the tune but there are no words.
The words are only speculation
(From the Latin speculum, mirror):
They seek and cannot find the meaning of the music.

JOHN ASHBERY, "Self-Portrait in a Convex Mirror"

In the *Three Studies for Self-Portrait*, 1983, Bacon moves to a less ferocious style. Bacon has said, "I loathe my own face, but I go on painting it only because I haven't got any other people to do. . . . One of the nicest things that Cocteau said was: 'Each day in the mirror I watch death at work.' This is what one does oneself." Bacon had to do himself because most of the others were dead: George Dyer, by suicide, Isabel Rawsthorne . . . And the late self-portraits bear the self-elegiac weight of loss. The physical dissolution stays, matter yielding to a flat impermeable surface; the central panel, least decayed, is most like a mask, a striking fraternity with the Blake life mask of 1955. And life masks are always funereal, death-in-life. But these dissolving presences are resigned, not furious. Bacon's vision of the life of the body was always harrowing, because he was a moralist in the classic rather than the colloquial sense. I think he may have more in common with Hogarth than with Lucian Freud.

In the *Triptych Inspired by the Oresteia of Aeschylus* (1981), it is the Bird Fury who is more sentient and wounded, an autobiographically suggestive frame. At other times, the Baconian world seems scourged, figures caught a moment after the Kindly Ones have retreated. We see the handiwork of Tisiphone, Alecto, Maegera; and it isn't just or unjustified, a stunningly capricious series of punishments (was Hitchcock's *The Birds*, with its wounded and wounding avengers, flying this same idea?). I have seen people in museums turn away from Bacon as though slapped, offended. This makes sense—which is to say, seems just. But to refuse to look at horror is a form of self-indulgence. "We didn't know," avoiding the truth, slant. The irony of Erinyes: to refuse to encounter horror is horrible; if you refuse the picture, you turn into it. And if you accept the truth of the image, you leave it unrelieved. There is an Epictetian balance in this small corner of the universe, taken one step further: a gray area between existentialism and nihilism—unsurprisingly by way of the stoics—between modernism and postmodernism. Epictetus said, according to Marcus Aurelius, "Thou art a little soul bearing about a corpse." His characterization of Epicurus: "This is the life of which you pronounce yourself worthy: eating, drinking, copulation, evacuation and snoring," which becomes Apeneck Sweeney's "Birth, and copulation, and death. / That's all the facts when you come to brass tacks: / Birth, and copulation, and death." Aeschylus, and Eliot, and Bacon.

~~~

We are returned to what we are: not quite fastened to a dying animal, we are the dying animal, gnawing at anything that fastens us to flesh, that of the self or of others, and confirming the animalism of our flesh by it. This is Bacon's "brutality of fact." The great "horror" of the paintings is in the initial violence of self-recognition, the wish to not be like what he says we are. Any moralism in Bacon's work enflames at the point at which we reject or close our eyes to who we are, our true self-image. And in this position of inauthenticity, we become doubly terrorized by our inability to do so. One critic recently called the world of Bacon's work "odious," an attempt to convict it of the charge of high distastefulness. I suppose he thought it should be locked away, where it could not do any harm. But all great grotesque art is realistic on some level; this is the source of its power. Fuseli's world, for example, is fanciful, thus not truly, not viscerally, grotesque. It does not risk authentic offensiveness.

~~~

. . . Is there anything
To be serious about beyond this otherness
That gets included in the most ordinary
Forms of daily activity, changing everything
Slightly and profoundly, and tearing the matter
Of creation, any creation, not just artistic creation
Out of our hands, to install it on some monstrous, near
Peak, too close to ignore, too far
For one to intervene? This otherness, this

"Not-being-us" is all there is to look at
In the mirror, though no one can say
How it came to be this way.

JOHN ASHBERY, "Self-Portrait in a Convex Mirror."

Bacon's self-portraits frequently remind me of the Zapruder film. Life goes forward and backward, toward a moment inevitable and enigmatic, corporifying the modern meaning of "tragic"; the worst that can happen is that the worst has happened and yields nothing transcendent.

Painters understand the problems of autobiography, self-portraiture, the plasticity of the self. Think of multiple self-portraits: Rembrandt, Van Gogh, Frida Kahlo, Jenny Saville . . . And in presenting the tenuous facticity of self as a fractious committee, in the *Three Studies* triptych, Francis Bacon, in the eighties, in his seventies, shows the face as a multiple choice, a challenge to sequentiality. Bacon's self in motion creates three moments of self-portrayal that formally discourage a single self-definition, not because they are interiorized but because they are so deeply antiarchetypal. We do not experience ourselves, specifically, in these selves but rather a more mysterious experience of self-experience, of self-contemplation—a posing of runic questions to our own dark hearts.

~~~

And still, and still . . . the center study is most composed, even though the full face is closed.

~~~

Bacon has said that he wanted to paint a mouth the way Monet painted a sunset. This late series, eyes mostly closed, mouth slightly open, is a great contrast to the early bestial teeth and primal screams of the popes and other anonymous human creatures. The lips are soft, slightly parted as though to inhale, as though to speak the trace of darkness showing through them, a trace the same shade as around the head. It is a rich surrounding blackness—almost hinting at the darkest brown—supple, aged, muffled. There is a restive silence in the near speech here. *Three Studies for Self-Portrait* is resolutely inward, the artist resolved into an enigmatic awe, as his dissolution reconstitutes into three versions of unchristian despair. Kurtz without the madness. What would he have said? A locution is passing through, articulated in dark colors, a comprehension of loss, an equivocal shantih.

~~~

The living wash in vain, in vain perfume themselves, they stink.

SAMUEL BECKETT, *First Love*

Health preserves life as such, in a sterile identity; while disease is an activity, the most intense a man can indulge in . . .

EMIL CIORAN, *A Short History of Decay*

If you can find a person totally without belief, but totally dedicated to futility, then you will find the more exciting person.

FRANCIS BACON, *The Brutality of Fact* (all subsequent quotations by Francis Bacon refer to this interview by David Sylvester, except where otherwise noted)

Well, now I'm glad to say that two people, very good-looking, have turned up. . . . Now I shall give up doing self-portraits.

FRANCIS BACON

Nature is corrupt. Without Christ man can only be vicious and wretched. With Christ man is free from vice and wretchedness. In him is all our virtue and all our happiness. Apart from him there is only vice, wretchedness, error, darkness, death, despair.

BLAISE PASCAL, *Pensées*, #416

I think that most people who have religious beliefs, who have the fear of God, are much more interesting than people who just live a kind of hedonistic and drifting life. On the other hand, I can't help admiring but despising them, living by a total falseness.

FRANCIS BACON

You must go on. I can't go on. I'll go on.

SAMUEL BECKETT, *The Unnameables*

We are born and we die, but in between we give this purposeless existence a meaning by our drives.

FRANCIS BACON

In spite of the sense that life is ultimately futile, nevertheless one finds the energy to do something which one believes in.

FRANCIS BACON

To be the descendant and namesake of the great lawyer-philosopher meant nothing to him; his family despaired of him.

LAWRENCE GOWING, "Francis Bacon: The Human Presence," in *Francis Bacon*

Certainly there is a consent between the body and the mind. . . . Therefore it is good to consider of deformity, not as a sign, which is more deceivable, but as a cause, which seldom faileth of the effect.

FRANCIS BACON, the great lawyer-philosopher, "Of Deformity"

I'm always hoping to deform people into appearance.

FRANCIS BACON

Of the human body itself, the eye sees only the surface, the skin; the inner body, however, is as much part of the idea.

FRIEDRICH NIETZSCHE, *Human, All Too Human*

I've also always had a book that's influenced me very much called *Positioning in Radiography*, with a lot of photographs showing the positioning of the body for the x-ray photographs to be taken, and the x-rays themselves.

FRANCIS BACON

The contemplative atheist is rare. . . . Great atheists indeed are hypocrites, which are ever handling holy things, but without feeling; so as they must needs be cauterized in the end.

FRANCIS BACON, the great lawyer-philosopher, "Of Atheism"

I've always been very moved by pictures about slaughterhouses and meat, and to me they belong very much to the whole thing of the Crucifixion. There've been extraordinary photographs which have been done of animals just being taken up before they were slaughtered; and the smell of death . . . they do everything to attempt to escape.

FRANCIS BACON

If I was in hell I would always feel I had a chance of escaping. I'd always be sure that I'd be able to escape.

FRANCIS BACON

~~~

But pure dust is the perfect colour for a grey suit.

FRANCIS BACON

~~~

Pure or impure, dust of any kind seems perfect for a gray face.

ON THE ART OF SURVIVAL

NORTH BY NORTHWEST

Everything has the color of those first photos of the moon, slightly unreal, so sharp we want to live in them forever, live forever in shades of blue and green, just sharp enough and bright enough and cool to the eyes. So perfect it almost hurts.

We start with a slanted world, the world told slant, a Caligarian modernism: midtown skyscrapers, our doubles—they mirror back motion as form and color. Vague taxis float along the lower surface. The building is an implacable mirror. So is advertising, which mirrors our desire. Bernard Herrmann's music: a spiraling Spanish jauntiness, as though in dancing so fast one were in danger of vertigo. But the camera is static; only the reflections move.

So if a man who has come from such a building, with an "O" in the middle of his name, were to shortly ask of his tormentor, a kind of personal anti-Christ, or perhaps a valet with too much power—a man as charming and debonair as he—if he were to ask in a moment of doubt, "Am I going to be dropped into a vat of molten steel and become part of some new skyscraper?" it shouldn't come as a shocking surprise that he is suffering from dramatic irony, a character flaw. But dramatic irony is almost always a cause for hope, as well. We think, "he doesn't know";

and we think, "but he might learn." And there is also cause for hope in his sardonic image of a skyscraper's body, with him feeding, like a transfusion, the body of glass and steel. (The prefigure of the Matrix? It's all the logic of late capitalism.) Let's say the tormentor is armed with a woman named Eve. We can't be headed for paradise, because it's after the Fall. And if such is the case and Eve still holds the forbidden fruit—knowledge he can't have—the way to somewhere else, where after all are we headed?

~~~

I have a kind of freakish, kooky grin when things go very wrong, finding funerals giddy and wake-like, even when the ceremony is solemn. At weddings, the weight of joy in the paradisiacal moment is usually more than I can bear. So.

I find myself moved more by comedy than by tragedy. You might ask, isn't this just the late-twentieth-, early-twenty-first-century predicament, our limited access to grand allegories? Certainly nothing is very new about the death of tragedy? To which I would respond, gentle straw person, that, well, yes. It's the Twentieth-Century Limited I'm on, headed north by northwest.

Or is it the Limited Twenty-First Century?

I'm in a generic wonderland, where supposed tragedies seem a bit silly—they're so big and I'm so small!—I go through the mirror and the scale isn't right.

Comedies, for me, are small stands on a precipice. We slip, or the rocks do—a pratfall followed by gestures of desperate recovery. Or a high wind comes along, a cosmic uh-oh. Changes in weather, changes in posture. Terrible things happen, and life normalizes; it rebounds. And it changes, if the comedy is to be more than static, or boring, or frivolous. An unexamined comedy, of course, may still be worth seeing, but it won't touch the deepest chords in the same way as *comedies noir*, with their surreal fortuities like a sequence of images from dreams. Think of a man hanging from a clock. A piano sliding down a long set of stairs. A man being chased by a plane in a cornfield.

Comedy and terror, a perfect recipe for the mid to late twentieth century, when, diminished and dislocated, we felt horrified that our small existences could stop on a dime through the intervention of death's enigmatic calibrations. People disappear. Diplomats are killed by umbrellas. Giant sinkholes. And oh, the placid fifties, when the anxiety in the American psyche starts bleeding out in violent noirs, alien invasion, monster movies, *Psycho, North by Northwest* . . . there is always a touch of the absurd, the surreal.

Hitchcock's art is related to Kafka's and Flannery O'Connor's. There is plenty of comedy, but limited relief. And chance is a moral subcategory.

Finding myself a rather absurd creature, perhaps I am only moved these days by absurd kin, or circumstance, by concordances of slapstick coincidence. Perhaps my art of survival is embedded in a comic mode ("He's in bed with the comic mode," I can hear them say).

In great comedies, no accident is purely accidental. Luck and misfortune are governed by choices that character, in both senses of the word, instigates.

Perhaps another word is necessary. What we call accident, in fact, is usually only partly so. Isabella Duncan's scarf was inadvertently wrapped around a tire. But it was not accidentally worn, nor did it fortuitously flap in the wind.

Grandmother's desire to turn down a road of misremembering, in "A Good Man Is Hard to Find," is not accidental. Nor is the appearance of the Misfit, completely. We know, after all, that he is about, if not completely what he is about. He must nevertheless show up somewhere, to someone.

In *The Trial*, Joseph K.'s fate is no more accidental than any other pawn's. It is merely improbable (in realistic terms) that on any given day any given person will meet the dark fate that the exigencies of character, culture, and politics necessitate. A good run of bad luck strains our sense of the probable, turning it into the absurd. At such moments we see ourselves as fictional.

It is not accidental that every corner has its historical accidents, its head-ons and near misses.

The grandmother, Joseph K, and Roger O. Thornhill, in their strategic withdrawals from authentic engagement and self-knowledge, in the size and quality, various again, of their egoism, are all headed for collisions with enigmatic Inquisitors: the Misfit, the Judge, Van Damm—antagonists who symbolize the extent of their moral culpability. It is the deictic function of the antagonists to attempt to force the protagonists, who mistake their disengagement for innocence, to see that they have fallen and that they are not victims.

Fortuity, actual and apparent, is the deus ex machina of *North by Northwest*. There should be another word for circumstance that aspires to the disastrous. An errant call to a bellboy, the broken wave of a hand, and one lands on the outskirts, just a few manicured miles from the city of Kafka. The implicit moral imperative in Hitchcock's films turns chance into a glass (of milk for example, lit from within) more than half-full of toxic rationalization. True of Kafka, enigmatically, and true of Flannery O'Connor, explicitly, accidents are made to happen, by the hand of the creator slapping a wrist, or slapping down a life too flawed to salvage, and the hand of a character provoking, invoking, his or her fate.

Black comedies are constructed from telling misconstructions. The beckoning gesture that seems to have no moral context: turn here, or come here—a command, an imprecation, a movement, a wave, a letter slipped under the door.

A name is announced in a crowded room. Do we rise and converge with our destiny, our accidental and fated intersection with our own heart of darkness? We must, since, after all, Mother might be waiting.

Hitchcock is the vengeful god as comedian. God makes his cameo appearance in the beginning of *North by Northwest*. The doors of a bus close in God's face.

~~~

Phillip Vandamm's—James Mason's—first words in the film: "Good evening," the Hitchcock trademark. Hitchcock, like O'Connor, is a vengeful god, a damning god, a god with a sadistic, a satanic streak. God, the dark provocateur.

Part of the great comedy in *North by Northwest* is the way Roger O. Thornhill, played by Cary Grant, all but leaps into the persona that his pursuers assume he possesses, partially because he needs to, partially because he is attracted to it. Everything is in the names.

EVE: What does the 'O' stand for?
THORNHILL: Nothing.

Thornhill is a bored and cynical man, emblemized by his use of the ROT monogram on his custom matchbook. Like O'Connor's characters, he must be tested: thus the thorns. He's the son of the man who missed the bus. As for his hill, it of course awaits him at the end of the film, in the form of those formidable cliffs of history and culture: Mount Rushmore.

If Thornhill is damned before he meets Van Damm, he'll even add the endorsement of his name to the lighting of the fires. He is in advertising—the selling of the soul—and twice divorced, with an overly attached mother, a sophisticated version of the Organization Man, the critique of which, as Barbara Ehrenreich notes in *Fear of Falling*, began almost as soon as he became perfected and widely duplicated in the midfifties. *North by Northwest* partakes of this critique and then poses that romantic myth that love can override the emptiness of *Homo economus*. Love kills cynicism.

The politics, I might add, are mostly a MacGuffin, though Hitchcock slyly incorporates both Cold War attitudes and a casually shocking—for the time—presentation of Cold Warrior callousness in the decision of the Leo G. Carroll–led operatives to sacrifice the innocent Thornhill to save their operation. Thornhill decides to challenge political loyalty for the sake of individual loyalty (saving Eve from her continuing role as operative whore). She can't get on that plane; the operation is compromised by the fact that she's met Thornhill on a higher plane.

~~~

In any case, the case of George Kaplan. I have always been puzzled by the use of "Kaplan," an overtly Jewish name. The plot is driven by Van Damm's desire (James Mason, playing a version of the Anglicized German, similar to Herbert Marshall in *Foreign Correspondent*), his need to kill the nonexistent agent,

Kaplan. Kaplan is the missing Jew, the nonexistent Jew, a joke from the pen of Ernest Lehmann, the scriptwriter. The spirit of postwar revenge, or a ghost of the diaspora? The cats chased by mice—metaphorically the hunting of Nazis by Jews after the war? It is by incorporating part of this nonexistent Jew into his character that Thornhill is able to disable the German. In becoming partly Jewish, he becomes a romantic idealist, discovering not only love but first love, the love that renews the world. In becoming the Jew, he can reemerge, cleansed of sloth, into a world where there are fewer Jews and no lingering Nazi types. A kind of paradise? The art of survival, apparently, is becoming a Jew, barely and briefly, and returning, not to a different world, but differently to the world.

~~~

What does a moment's confusion—the wrong name on a slip of paper handed to the wrong man with the long scar that dips across his face like a scythe, like a new forbidding constellation that never leaves the sky, or a glimpse of encircling hands, let's say through a cracked door the wind has leaned against, in a building one has entered looking for a half-remembered office of a misplaced friend, or better yet a call to a busboy looking for a man who is being looked for, which attaches to us a name, a state of affairs, a fate, if you will—what does a contingency of mistaken identity have to do with our guiltiness, sinfulness, gracelessness? Nothing, everything, when one's middle name is "Nothing."

~~~

Last week I woke up and browsed the *Times*, barely awake. The obituaries: George Kaplan, investment banker, dead at fifty-eight. "But I'm George Kaplan," I thought. "And the irony is that I can't be dead, because I never existed." My confused mis-apprehensions in the twenty minutes or so after sleep are inev-itably more disturbing, more surreal, bred closer to the bone of who I may or may not be than any dreams I recall, pick apart, and throw in the yard for the pigs of the unconscious to root around and devour. I woke up a little more, came slowly back to life.

Once in New York, I passed a woman on the street who gave me a nice sidelong glance, a kind of leering interest, I thought. We turned around at the same time, as though we were play-ing Harpo Marx meets Baudelaire, and she came toward me and put her hand on my arm. "Didn't you go out with Carol Johnson a few years ago?" she asked me. It was sixty degrees, late in an April afternoon—you know, the kind of weather where you're all there and all but disappear, when you think you could be anyone if you weren't who you were—and I said no, no, and she withdrew her hand and we backed away from each other, smirking, and both thinking, I believe, that I should have been who she thought I was, but both were in a motion too light and propelling to deny or assert too assiduously. What might have beens, the Harpo-honking of the taxis on Park Avenue. I think of Carol Johnson all the time. But in my mind she's married to George Kaplan now.

~~~

In the Room of My Mistaken Identity

In the bedroom of my double who doesn't exist
The coats are limp in the closet
Everything is so neat you could see a pin drop
The light in the bathroom is always on

The windows are always closed
This other life suits me with such near perfection
Even my mother would swear it was me

~~~

Hitchcock is a Catholic Freudian, in extremis. Father is missing. Father is never mentioned. Mother is disapproving. Mother is too close. Mother has tickets for the theater. Mother can be bribed to get a hotel room number. Mother is dubious about our avowed truths, seeing them as another car in a long train of discrepancies. Mother can't be reached; she has no phone. But still we try to reach her. We are always trying to reach Mother. We signal for the bellboy. We have a message for Mother. This sets our confused identity in motion. If we didn't know better, we'd say the mistake is Mother's. Mother joins Father as a missing person, once the train is in motion. We never see Mother again.

~~~

In this story, Eve started with betrayal, her eyes lighting on the first man she saw in the narrow corridor.

Having eaten, she leaned across the linen, as the world passed by, a blur of houses, trees, skies. That's what much of life is anyhow. The world is generic when we pluck the knowledge of our own unimportance, down from the tree of egos. But when we bite, the taste of ids is sweet and pulpy. Trees, houses, skies. The world passed by at a pace that didn't change. The talk was sexy after she had eaten.

The berth is open, the time is day, the light fading, the train on time. No one moves to keep oneself whole. One only moves to make oneself a motion, out of which a new gesture may emerge. Sewn into the pockets of his newest gabardine is a word he can't remember, a name he can't use.

~~~

So much depends
Upon a redcap
Gliding through the station,
Its gray-flannel passengers
Dancing to white noise

~~~

A car emerges from a cornfield. Two men face each other across a dusty road. They're dark suited and perplexed, as though they had a sudden flash that facing each other across the highway were two suits, a reflection of one man reduced to fiber and fabric. A biplane dusts crops *where there ain't no crops to dust*. It's a scene from Magritte, like the multitudes of men in suits, floating in a flat blue sky. The surreal's a kind of accidental beauty, half-ridiculous and half-threatening, just like any other dream. Nothing is where it's supposed to be, and it's all just right. The art of survival is seeing the man see a plane, and then seeing the plane. And the art of survival is seeing the plane despite the fact that the image pulls back, resists while it assures you that you're not exactly wrong. And the art of survival is running from something that slips out of the sky, that doesn't make sense but condenses all the fears we've ever held and tried to shake. It's a dream so large it could fill a childhood. The dreamer in this scene is a man on the ground, a man with a camera, a man watching the screen from the safety of his chair. But anyone awake in the dark or asleep in the day senses that the dreamer has an X on his back; he can only run hard in that timeless space and flat time, when the dark wings pick up speed and descend at midday, zeroing in on us, like a toy holocaust whose remote control is shattered.

~~~

I don't know if I'm Kaplan (Chaplin? Chaplain?) or Thornhill. When mistakes of identity occur, life takes on a strangely tautological air. We introduce ourselves to those who already know us, who laugh at our disclaimers with the laugh of those who should have known we would say just that. No, no, I'm really not who you think. Of course, of course, they say, just like you to keep the joke going. It's no joke, we say. They respond, you're just as funny as we remember, and not quite funny enough.

~~~

Is Eve is my Magdalene, thinking she fucks the good fight? Or am I the tramp, the wrong man in the right place at the wrong time, forever falling down, forever getting up. Perhaps I have known too little. They made her know too much. Still and all, she couldn't have known, when she sent me to a field and an open road, that she would never have sent me there feeling as she came to feel.

~~~

EVE: I did treat you miserably . . .
THORNHILL   (A SELF-ACCUSATION): I hated you for it . . .
EVE   (FALTERING): And I didn't want you to . . .
                  go on . . . thinking . . .
THORNHILL   (SOFTENING SLIGHT): I used some pretty
                  harsh words. I'm . . . sorry . . .
EVE: They hurt . . . deeply . . .

THORNHILL (DEFENSIVELY): Naturally, if I'd known . . .
EVE (DEFENSIVELY): I couldn't tell you . . .
THORNHILL: Of course not.
EVE: Could I?
THORNHILL: No, I guess not.
EVE: You didn't get hurt. I'm so relieved.
THORNHILL (EAGERLY): Of course I was hurt. How
        would you have felt if ——?
EVE: I mean in the cafeteria when you fell. When I
        shot you with the blanks.

Perhaps we're at our most poignant in uttering incomplete sentences. Not knowing where the words can go, or not able to go with the words. A man and a woman standing with a stand of trees between them. What do they want to say, as the man moves through the trees; he is confused, as though the trees were moving through his mind, as though each tree were a word with a ring of possibilities, going back to each word's first germination. This time their words brush, as her own trees feel the wind of his desire. They both feel the vicious circles behind the bark of what may be the wrong trees.

~~~

Black Hills. Familiar faces that alienate with features gorged from stone. Rows of lights in a sudden clearing.

A man's shadow passes over a TV screen.

To learn that our fear was inspired by a gun full of blanks.

But nothing is more exhilarating than running with someone away from certain death.

We stand on a granite ledge, telling each other to hold on.

Someone looking down, someone looking up.

History is faceless when the great faces of men are really just environmental ottomans, support for the feet that can't stay put. A hand reaches down. Whose is it—who is he? A hand reaches up. Who am I trying to save? For that matter, who am I, just trying not to fall, to think the extended hand might lift me to an upper berth? But in this story, we started with the fallen world, the true first state of things.

Bodies slip over the edge, leaving history, leaving us to our own devices.

A foot slips on history's stone face, a hand pulling down, a hand pulling up. From certain death in a hard spinning fall, to love and sex and finally the berth. It could be worse. It has been.

After all, in this story, we end in paradise. Comedies supposedly end with marriage; tragedies, with death. We end heading east, south by southeast.

ACKNOWLEDGMENTS

I'd like to thank the editors of the journals and anthologies in which some of the essays in this collection first appeared:

"Calling for His Past," *Southwest Review* 75, no. 3:406–11.

"Across the River," *Arts & Letters* 12 (Fall 2004): 39–45.

"The City Always Speaks," *Ocean State Review* 2, no. 1 (Summer 2012): 164–72.

"The Coat," *Mississippi Valley Review* 22, no. 1 (1996): 49–55.

"Occasional Desire: On the Essay and the Memoir," *Pleiades* 25, no. 2 (2005): 35–49. Subsequently published in David Lazar, ed., *Truth in Nonfiction* (Iowa City: University of Iowa Press, 2008). Originally delivered in a slightly shorter form at the Chautauqua Institution, Chautauqua NY, 2006.

"Reading New Year's Eve," in *Understanding the Essay*, ed. Patricia Foster and Jeff Porter (Peterborough ON: Broadview Press, 2012), 206–17.

"The Useable Past of M. F. K. Fisher," *Southwest Review* 77, no. 4:515–31.

"On Mentorship," *Ohio Review*, no. 51 (1995): 25–33.

"On Dating," in *Metawritings: Toward a Theory of Nonfiction*, ed. Jill Balbot (Iowa City: University of Iowa Press, 2012), 47–59.

"Death, Death, Death, Death, Death," special issue, edited by David Shields, *Seattle Review* 2, nos. 2–3 (2010): 179–91.

"Self-Portrait: Francis Bacon's Deformity," in "Sheer Painting/
Poetry," special issue, *Denver Quarterly* 28, no. 1 (Summer
1993): 83–89.

"On the Art of Survival: *North by Northwest*," *Denver Quarterly*
30, no. 4 (Spring 1996): 121–31.

"Calling for His Past" and "The Coat" were named Notable
Essays of the Year by *Best American Essays*.

Kristen Elias Rowley, my editor at Nebraska, was a wonderfully
patient and excellent shepherd for this project. I'm also grateful for
the unwavering support of the following friends: Celeste Wiser,
Martin McGovern, Alyce Miller, Lois Zamora, Stephen Zamora,
Susan Larsen, Christina Peters, Lia Purpura, Mary Cappello,
Adam McOmber, Cathleen Calbert, and Scott Lazar, and to my
father and stepmother, Leo and Roz Lazar. Patrick Madden,
crucially for this book, and Shannon Lakanen, Desirae Matherly,
and Mike Danko continually have reminded me why this work has
been important to me, as have so many of my current and former
students. I would also like to thank Steve Zuckerman for many
priceless conversations.

To my most ardent supporter, Delmore Lazar, this book is dedicated.

CPSIA information can be obtained at www.ICGtesting.com
Printed in the USA
LVOW130938030713

341341LV00001B/3/P